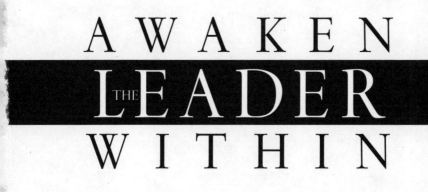

AWAKEN THE LEADER WITHIN

AWAKEN
THE LEADER
WITHIN

How the Wisdom
of Jesus
Can Unleash Your Potential

ZondervanPublishingHouse
Grand Rapids, Michigan 49530
http://www.zondervan.com

Awaken the Leader Within

Requests for information should be addressed to:

 ZondervanPublishingHouse
Grand Rapids, Michigan 49530

Library of Congress Cataloging-in-Publication Data

Perkins, Bill, 1949-
    Awaken the leader within: how the wisdom of Jesus can unleash your potential /
Bill Perkins.
      p. cm.
    Includes bibliographical references.
    ISBN: 0-310-23087-X (alk. paper)
    1. Christian leadership. I. Title.
BV652.1 .P43 2000
253–dc 21
                                          00-023559
                                               CIP

This edition is printed on acid-free paper.

All Scripture quotations, unless otherwise indicated, are taken from the *Holy Bible:
New International Version*®. NIV®. Copyright © 1973, 1978, 1984 by International
Bible Society. Used by permission of Zondervan Publishing House. All rights reserved.

Published in association with Wolgemuth and Associates, Inc., 8600 Crestgate Circle,
Orlando, FL 32819.

Interior design by Amy E. Langeler

Printed in the United States of America

00 01 02 03 04 05/❖ DC/ 10 9 8 7 6 5 4 3 2 1

*To Bob Bobosky, who continually surprises me
with his vision and grace.*

ACKNOWLEDGMENTS

*J*n appreciation to

... my loving wife, Cindy, and my three sons, Ryan, David, and Paul. They have always supported me and encouraged me in my labor.

... the wonderful people of South Hills Community Church, who have urged me to take the time needed for this book. I'm especially grateful to Bob and Mary Ann Noack, Dave and Judy Carr, Steve Wilent, Bart Hafeman, and Mark Hollis.

... Brad Nydahl, who read and critiqued some of the early chapters and pointed me toward some excellent resources; Lane Kagey, who also provided me with some resource material; and Mike Quisling, who read and critiqued the entire manuscript.

... my agent, Robert Wolgemuth and his associates, Jennifer Cortez and David Dunham, who helped shape the idea for the book.

... Lyn Cryderman and Dirk Buursma, along with the other wonderful people at Zondervan Publishing House, who had a vision for a book that would help people discover how the wisdom of Jesus could unleash the leader within them.

... the many leaders whose stories are mentioned in this book. I gratefully recognize their contribution to this work and apologize for anyone I may have unintentionally failed to acknowledge.

I'm especially thankful to God for giving me a message of hope.

CONTENTS

PART TWO: AWAKEN YOUR SKILLS

PART ONE

AWAKEN YOUR CHARACTER

*The good man brings good things out of
the good stored up in him.*

JESUS OF NAZARETH—MATTHEW 12:35

1

TURN YOUR POTENTIAL LOOSE

Former United States president Dwight D. Eisenhower defined leadership as "the art of getting someone else to do something you want done because he wants to do it." If you accept this definition of leadership (it happens to be my favorite), then you're buying into two truths. The first is this: You're a leader. Typically when I make that observation at business seminars, I'm greeted with looks of disbelief. Undaunted, I ask the audience a very simple question: "Have you ever been in a situation at work or home where you tried to get someone else to do something?" Immediately everyone raises their hand and nods their head.

According to Eisenhower's definition, you become a leader the moment you attempt to get someone else to do something. Given the accuracy of the definition, the issue isn't, "Are you a leader?" You are! The issue is, "How can you lead more effectively?"

Asking that question leads us to a second truth issuing out of Eisenhower's definition, namely, that leaders are made, not born. Because leadership is an art, effective leadership is the result of hard work—not good genes. So whether you've recently been propelled into a leadership role and feel as out of place as a turtle at a road race, or you're heading up a Fortune 500 company, there are certain things you need to do to sharpen your leadership skills.

You become a leader the moment you attempt to get someone else to do something.

Learning to lead is like learning to master a musical instrument—there are fundamental chords that can be studied, practiced, and mastered. I've discovered it doesn't matter whether I'm meeting with the chief executive officer of a billion-dollar company about business strategies, or counseling a mother or father about strategies of child-rearing—the fundamentals of leadership are the same and must be mastered. While natural talent is a shortcut to musical excellence, to possess that talent doesn't negate the necessity of hard work. Similarly, while some men and women have a natural capacity for leadership, they too must study the art and work hard at mastering the fundamentals. Those with less innate talent can still excel as leaders if they're willing to study the basic principles and put them into practice.

Becoming an effective leader demands rigorous study and hard work. I didn't write this book for the purpose of providing you with feel-good fluff to help you make it through the day. It's not intended to serve as an injection of fantasy faith, like Dorothy in *The Wizard of Oz,* who flew home after clicking her heels together and saying, "There's no place like home." The leadership style of Jesus, which serves as the basis for this book's teaching, isn't based on fantasy, positive thinking, or feel-goodism. It's based on a life that demonstrated honesty, vision, sacrifice, and love.

In just three and a half years Jesus established a movement that has lasted twenty centuries and inspired billions of people. He did this without traveling far from home, writing a book, leading an army, or holding a political office.

How did one man so significantly influence the world? He did it by personally training individuals and utilizing techniques we can study, practice, and eventually master. His strategy wasn't the result of a lucky toss of the dice but of a well-thought-out plan by a man with sterling character and finely honed leadership skills. He didn't succeed because he recruited a team of superstars, but because he passed on to his team the character traits and skills they in turn would need to pass on to others.

This book is written for the man or woman who wants to lead like Jesus.

Jesus didn't sanction the separation of character and competence in a leader. In fact, his harshest words were aimed at leaders who looked competent on the outside but were rotten on the inside.

Having said that, I want you to know I'm not writing this book from the perspective of someone who has reached the pinnacle of success and from my lofty vantage point am telling you how to get where I am. I know what it's like to lead a fast-growing organization—and I know what it's like to lead with failure staring me in the face. In most respects I'm still looking forward to the realization of my dreams. It is in this sense that I've become at least somewhat skilled at leading when times are tough and rewards are minimal.

This book is written for the man or woman who wants to lead like Jesus—those who believe that character counts just as much as competence and who consequently want to develop both. If you're that kind of a leader, then buckle your seat belt because you're in for a ride that will unleash your potential. In the first half of the book you'll discover how the wisdom of Jesus can awaken the character of a leader within you; in the remainder of the book you'll examine how Jesus applied six crucial leadership skills and how you can learn to practice and master them.

I've tried to draw on the best leadership literature available to translate the wisdom of Jesus into practical and usable

15

terms. I'm going to share insights I've gained as I've conducted leadership seminars around the country, met with business leaders, and served as pastor of a church.

As you read, search for a few principles you can immediately put into practice. Remind yourself each time you pick up the book that small changes over a long period of time will take you in the end to a radically better place. Each of us is like a plane leaving an airport—a mere two percent change in trajectory at takeoff in Los Angeles will take the plane to a radically different place two thousand miles away. And if the wisdom of Jesus enables you to become two percent more like him in your leadership style, you will surely take those you lead to a better place over the course of the next year.

∞

THE WISDOM OF JESUS

- Jesus led with honesty, vision, sacrifice, and love.

- Jesus intentionally utilized leadership techniques we can study, practice, and master.

- Jesus urged his team to follow his example.

2

WEAR NO MASKS

*I*t was a simple question, and I expected a quick answer. As the chief executive officer of the company that built Seattle's Space Needle, Brad was known to be quick on his feet.

But when I asked the question, he paused, tilted his head to one side, placed his hand on his chin, and contemplated an answer.

"Leaders of integrity?" he mused out loud.

Finally he looked me in the eye and said, "I know a man who has integrity in every area of his life." And then Brad hesitated as something came to his mind. "Well, there is one area where he lacks integrity—he's political and tells people what they want to hear in order to keep his options open."

He paused again and said, "And then there's a man I know who lives in New York. He has integrity in business—always keeps his promises." Once more he paused and then whispered, "He cheats on his wife though."

"Bill, I don't think I know a leader who possesses integrity in *every* area of his life. At least not once I get to know them better."

17

Before he could continue his thought I interrupted. "What about you? You've got integrity, don't you?"

Is integrity, like a rainbow, something we can chase but never catch? Or is our understanding of integrity so limited that we don't understand exactly what it is and how to acquire it?

Brad lifted an eyebrow and said, "Yes, except in one area."

"What's that?"

"I care for people, but I have a hot temper."

My conversation with Brad took place a few hours ago, and I'm still struggling with the implication of his words—"I don't think I know a leader who possesses integrity in *every* area of his life."

Are there no leaders of integrity among us? Is integrity, like a rainbow, something we can chase but never catch? Or is our understanding of integrity so limited that we don't understand exactly what it is and how to acquire it?

These are important questions because the people you lead want you to possess integrity. In fact, after researchers James Kouzes and Barry Posner surveyed thousands of people and performed more than four hundred case studies, they discovered that people value honesty and integrity in a leader more than anything else. Virtually every person they talked with placed integrity at the top of their leadership wish list.[1]

Integrity is the foundation on which your leadership will stand or fall. No matter whether you lead a company, a church, a family, a battalion, or an athletic team—those you lead want to know they can trust you. They want to follow you without fear of disappointment.

INTEGRITY DEFINED

A biblical writer once wrote, "Jesus Christ is the same yesterday and today and forever."[2] Jesus is both eternal and unchanging. If the author of Hebrews had wanted to use one word to describe Jesus as unchanging he could have said, "Jesus possesses *integrity*." The word *integrity* speaks of someone who is "whole, or complete" and has the same root word as does the word *integrated*.[3] Leaders of integrity have taken the principles that govern their lives (principles like the biblical Ten Commandments) and internalized them, integrating them into every area of their lives.

Leaders of integrity aren't like a weather vane that changes direction with every shift of the social winds. They are like a compass that is internally magnetized so it

Integrity is the foundation on which your leadership will stand or fall. Those you lead want to know they can trust you.

always points true north regardless of what's happening around it. They are honest at work *and* at home. They keep promises *even* if it means a financial loss. They speak well of their clients in their presence *and* behind their backs. They don't treat their spouses with respect in public and belittle them behind closed doors. Leaders of integrity don't switch masks to win the favor of the audience to which they're playing.

Because leaders of integrity don't pretend to be something they're not, what you see is what you get—literally. And it's not that leaders of integrity are perfect—surely they aren't. But they are aware of their weaknesses and don't want to lead others to believe they have no personal flaws. When my friend Brad admitted that he cared for people but had a hot temper, while he may not have realized it, his statement demonstrated integrity.

As we finished our lunch, Brad said, "You know, Bill, only one man possessed perfect integrity." He's right, of course. And if we're going to lead effectively, we need to let the example of Jesus show us what integrity looks like and how it can be cultivated in our lives.

A CLOSER LOOK

Nobody who endured the Watergate hearings (1972–1974) will forget listening to the recorded conversations between

President Richard Nixon and his closest advisers. Behind closed doors the president spewed forth obscenities like a seasoned sailor. The more we listened the more we realized Nixon's public and private personas were radically different.

Of course, Nixon is by no means alone. In an effort to keep his "private" life private, President Bill Clinton lied about his relationship with Monica Lewinsky. "Who wouldn't lie about an affair?" one news commentator asked, implying that we should not only accept such lying but should in fact expect it from a leader under such circumstances.

The seemingly unending stream of scandalous information about national leaders has become so routine many are insisting that we declare the private life of a leader as "off-limits." Some insist, "As long as he gets the job done, it doesn't matter what he does in private."

Jesus didn't endorse that philosophy. One day while walking along the shore of the Sea of Galilee, he saw two fishermen casting their nets. He waved an arm and told the men to follow him. Immediately Peter and Andrew left their nets, their boats, and their fishing business—and they followed Jesus.[4] For the next three and a half years they were as close to Jesus as his shadow. The man who led them pulled open the curtains of his private life and invited them to look inside.

AN INTEGRATED ETHIC

Because leaders of integrity consistently live out their ethic (their set of moral principles or values), they aren't afraid of scrutiny. In 1836 Abraham Lincoln was campaigning for election to the Illinois legislature when his opponent, Robert Allen, publicly claimed that he possessed evidence of corruption that would destroy Lincoln's credibility. Allen promised to keep the details confidential as a favor to Lincoln. Of course, the mere *mention* of impropriety had the potential to so soil Lincoln's reputation that he could very well lose the election.

Instead of mopping his brow and sighing in relief that Allen was willing to keep the details to himself, Lincoln sent a letter to Allen with this exhortation: "That I once had the confidence of the people of Sangamon, is sufficiently evident, and if I have since done anything, either by design or misadventure, which if known would subject me to a forfeiture of that confidence, he that knows of that thing, and conceals it, is a traitor to his country's interest."[5]

Because leaders of integrity consistently live out their ethic, they aren't afraid of scrutiny.

As a leader of integrity Lincoln wasn't afraid of exposure—in fact, he insisted that Allen bring forth every dirty fact regardless of the consequences he would suffer. Lincoln didn't fear exposure, because there was nothing to expose.

One thing that repeatedly frustrated Jesus' enemies was their inability to catch him doing something wrong. While Jesus often disregarded their customs and ignored their prejudices, they never heard him lie or saw him cheat. He consistently practiced the highest standard of ethics. He once said, "Do not think that I have come to abolish the Law or the Prophets; I have not come to abolish them but to fulfill them."[6] Jesus could look at the entire moral code of the Old Testament, including the Ten Commandments, and say with total honesty, "Those are the ethics I hold to, and throughout the course of my life I have kept them perfectly." On one occasion he asked his enemies, "Can any of you prove me guilty of sin?"[7] And while the community's most brilliant legal experts followed Jesus around, looking for some infraction of the law, they never found a single one!

If you want to be a leader of integrity you need to integrate your ethic into *every* area of your life. You don't want to be like the church leader who told me he practiced the "One-Hundred-Mile Rule." When I asked him to explain the rule, he said, "When I'm in town I conform to the rules of the church. But when I'm a hundred miles away I can do whatever I want." Ultimately his double life was uncovered, and his nationally acclaimed ministry plummeted to the ground like a wounded bird.

Because leaders of integrity integrate their ethic into every area of their lives, they possess a second characteristic—one a high school football coach from Massachusetts desperately needed.

AUTHENTICITY

For over twenty years William "Nick Eddy" McMullen served as an assistant coach at Old Colony High School in New Bedford, Massachusetts. The head coach and the student athletes were thrilled to have him coaching football at Old Colony. After all, Eddy was a former Notre Dame running back and a Heisman trophy finalist in 1966, who then went on to play for the Detroit Lions in the National Football League.

For twenty years nobody knew the truth about McMullen. And what was the truth? He was an impostor. His ruse would have continued if he hadn't agreed to meet with a fan who knew the real Eddy—a man who had met the football star when McMullen played for Notre Dame. One look—and the fan realized that this fellow claiming to be McMullen was in reality a pretender. The real Eddy is six feet two inches tall and weighs two hundred pounds-plus, while the impostor stood five feet seven inches tall and weighed 160 pounds.

The fan telephoned the real Eddy, who then called the charlatan and urged him to come clean. "I told him he could stop looking over his shoulder, waiting for the phone to ring."[8]

While few leaders would go so far as to assume the name and history of another person, all of us give false impressions. In an effort to strengthen our credibility we communicate an exaggerated level of honesty, care, commitment, and knowledge. We pretend our strained marriages are healthy and our voracious appetites are under control. How often has a chief executive officer or a head coach promised to remain with a company or team only to abandon ship for a higher-paying, more prestigious job? How often have political leaders made promises no man or woman could possibly deliver on? How often has a religious leader condemned the sins of others and later been caught committing the very same sins?

Because leaders of integrity have integrated their ethic into every area of their lives, they communicate authentically with those they lead. They don't pretend to be someone they aren't. Because they speak honestly and openly about their strengths and weaknesses, people trust them.

Toward the end of his life Jesus told his disciples, "Anyone who has seen me has seen the Father."[9] In essence he was saying, "When you look at me you're looking at God."

His claim would have been ludicrous except for the fact that everything he ever said and did substantiated his declaration. That's why Peter could confidently identify him as the Messiah—"the Christ, the Son of the living God."[10]

But remember, Jesus not only identified himself as the Son of God, but as the Son of Man. Peter not only saw Jesus walk on water, but he also saw him weep at the grave of Lazarus and heard him cry out in agony in Gethsemane. Jesus was authentic about his divinity *and* humanity. He allowed his disciples to see him as both God and man.

> *Because leaders of integrity have integrated their ethic into every area of their lives, they communicate authentically with those they lead.*

If I'm going to lead with integrity, not only will I consistently practice my ethic in every area of my life, but I'll also be honest about who I am. When I interviewed for my second pastorate, I told the members of the church, "I'll consistently provide you with biblical messages that are insightful, entertaining, and practical. I'll challenge the men to a deeper devotion to God, and I'll help the church grow."

Those are the kinds of things churches love to hear. But I also said, "You need to know I'm not detail oriented, and my pastoral gifts of counseling and comforting aren't very strong." I made it clear that if they were looking for a man who would hand out warm fuzzies to each parishioner, they needed to look elsewhere for their next pastor.

I don't particularly like pointing out my weaknesses to others—but because I'm committed to authenticity, I refuse to pretend I'm someone I'm not. I want those I lead to know I'm the same on the inside as I appear on the outside. I'm sure you want that too. But if you know yourself well, you realize that you're pretty skilled at hiding what's on the inside. You've got a closet full of masks you can put on to fit a vast variety of situations—all so you'll look better than you are. We all do.

While most of us realize we hide behind masks, it's especially painful when we're faced with the choice of continuing to hide or letting others see the truth. A number of years ago I realized I had lied to a team of people I led. At the time, I convinced myself it wasn't a lie at all—just a convenient omission. As I reflected on what I had done, I was especially troubled, because I thought lying was a problem *other* leaders had. I was afraid to confess my misdeed, because to do so might sacrifice the trust and loyalty of my team.

What would a leader of integrity do when he realized he had lied?

On the outside I was appearing to be spiritual and courageous, but on the inside I was scrambling to justify what I had done. I had a hard time accepting the fact that I, an essentially honest man, had lied. More than anything I wanted to pretend I *never* exaggerated or distorted the truth for my advantage. I wanted to be seen as a *perfect* leader who deserved the unquestioning devotion of my followers. The question I had to ask myself was this: "What would a leader of integrity do when he realized he had lied?" It took every ounce of resolve I possessed to peel back the mask and reveal the ugly man hiding underneath it. I found it a whole lot easier to *talk* about the value of authenticity than to *practice* it—especially when to do so required revealing a personal flaw. As is often the case, my fears were worse than the reality. When I admitted what I had done, those I talked with assured me of their understanding and continued support.

As leaders it's easy to believe that those under our supervision are better off with the illusion of perfection than with the raw, unvarnished truth about us. When I was in high school, the father of one of my best friends was Charlie Rivers, a well-known television commentator in central Texas. His youthful face, thick brown hair, and warm smile made him one of the most-recognized and best-loved men in Austin. I'll never forget the first time I saw him off-camera in the privacy of his home—Charlie had no hair!

Like Charlie Rivers, leaders often pretend to be something they're not. Nobody these days cares if a television personality wears a hairpiece, but it's a different issue when a leader pretends to be something he or she isn't. Eventually those internal flaws will surface, like dandelion seeds coming to fruition in lush grass, and when they do, inauthentic leaders will hasten to try to cover the flaws or discredit the person who pointed them out.

THE CULTIVATION OF INTEGRITY

I believe our tendency to hide is the greatest enemy we face in the development of integrity. Fear is a word that was never used in reference to Jesus. He was never afraid one of his disciples would see his humanity and conclude he couldn't possibly be God and man.

Our problem is this: We know a gap exists between our ethic and our behavior. Nobody, except Jesus, was a moral "perfect ten." And that's the rub; we feel we *should be* a "ten," and therefore we are desperate to give that impression.

I chuckle every time I think of the story in which a man died and stood at the gate of heaven. As he waited in line to get in, an angel handed him a hundred-pound stick of chalk and told him to climb a ladder that ascended far up into space and mark a rung for each sin he had committed during his life. After he had been climbing for several months—and the piece of chalk was just a tiny sliver in his hand—he cried out in pain when somebody stepped on his hand. He looked up and saw Mother Teresa of Calcutta.

"What are you doing?" he yelled.

"I'm going down for more chalk," she replied.

I like that story because it illustrates the fact that even the most revered and seemingly holy leader does not and cannot perfectly measure up to Jesus. And as leaders we fear that we will lose our influence if we allow those under our charge to see our flaws.

We can strengthen our integrity by admitting that we overestimate how faithfully we cultivate it.

The men Jesus trained to advance his cause were no different from you and me. They pledged allegiance to a high moral ethic that they repeatedly violated, and they were often out of touch with their personal shortcomings. They too tried to hide their weaknesses behind a variety of masks—and more often than not they denied their weaknesses even existed.

Of course, it's one thing to admit our tendency to hide behind a mask of some sort and another thing to throw that mask away once and for all. Unfortunately, the reality is that many leaders will violate their set of moral principles or values if the reward is high enough. Ironically, we can strengthen our integrity by admitting that we overestimate how faithfully we cultivate it. I believe we *must* identify gaps between our ethic and our behavior if we're going to become leaders of integrity. To put it another way, we must know our weaknesses and fortify them.

WOULD YOU VIOLATE YOUR ETHIC?

You may have found that last paragraph a bit troubling. "I would never compromise my ethic, my set of moral principles and values," you may say. Really? Perhaps you need to reconsider. On the night before Jesus' crucifixion, the Lord told Peter that he would disown Jesus three times. Peter said, "Even if I have to die with you, I will never disown you."[11]

Peter professed the highest, the most commendable, of all human principles and values. He said he would go so far as to die for Jesus. A few hours later, however, he did exactly as Jesus predicted he would do: He disowned Jesus three times. With each denial Peter proved that his behavior did not measure up to his avowed ethic.

Jesus knew that Peter would one day lead the church—but he also knew that the fisherman would disown him. Yet even that knowledge did not undermine the Lord's confidence in Peter's leadership ability. Shortly before predicting the apostle's denial of him, Jesus said, "When you have turned back, strengthen your brothers."[12]

Peter discovered on that dreadful night that he loved himself more than Jesus. He learned he wasn't the man of integrity he believed himself to be. That reality proved so painful for Peter that he sought solace in his original vocation. The apostle John brings that to our attention when he tells how, after Jesus had appeared following the resurrection, Peter declared to the other disciples that he was "going out to fish."[13]

Peter must have wondered how a man like himself, one who possessed so little integrity, could ever again be of service to the Lord. What he would soon discover was that Jesus looks not for perfect leaders, but for men and women who hold to his high ethic and who seek to flesh it out in their lives. He wants leaders who are so committed to integrity that they allow others to bring it to their attention when they exaggerate, break a promise, make a promise that cannot be fulfilled, or compromise the truth for personal advantage.

Jesus looks not for perfect leaders, but for men and women who hold to his high ethic and who seek to flesh it out in their lives.

History tells us that Peter, so beautifully reinstated by Jesus,[14] went on to be one of the pillars of the early church. In his two letters to first-century Christians, he wrote of humility, forgiveness, and personal holiness. He became a leader of integrity, to be sure, but he never became perfect—remember, that's a description reserved for Jesus. Even as the church grew and his leadership role expanded, Peter remained open to the rebuke of those who spotted inconsistency in his life.[15]

Similarly, you would be well served to ask God, and a few trusted friends as well, to bring to your attention instances

27

where you haven't acted, or aren't acting, with integrity. And as a leader you'll want to gently do the same for those you lead.

Avoid Hypocrisy

Several years ago an influential leader in the church I pastored told me that he felt I needed a softer touch in the way I dealt with people. He observed that my rough, abrasive style needed to be smoothed out if I was going to become an effective leader.

Of course, he wasn't the first person to point out that flaw in my social style. Many others, including my wife, best friends, children, coaches, parents, neighbors, teammates, staff members, and mail carriers, had helped me realize I needed to be more sensitive when making a decision or pointing out a mistake in someone else.

In this particular case the problem wasn't my lack of awareness in this area—I *knew* I needed to become more sensitive— it was that the man who confronted me had, at least in my mind, a bigger problem than my own. I had heard him verbally blast subordinates. On several occasions I had been the target of such an outburst.

One day as we ate lunch in my office I asked him, "Dan, have you ever considered the possibility that one reason you're so troubled by my insensitivity to other people is because it's a problem you struggle with yourself?"

He immediately became incensed. His face flushed; his muscles tightened. He locked his jaw, clenched his teeth, and spat out, "I am not like you in this area." He was so offended by my suggestion that a short time later he left the church. The pain of facing this imperfection drove him to sweep under the rug of his conscious mind all awareness of it. Even when his closest friends tried to help him face this weakness, he refused to listen. As much as I loved, and still love, him, this man was a hypocrite in that area of his life. He held to a high ethic of sensitivity, which he didn't always practice. I suspect, as you read these words, you could bring to mind numerous leaders you know who are just like my friend—leaders who deny weaknesses in their character or personality style that are so obvious to everyone around them that they could just as well be wearing an obvious mask.

JESUS' HARSHEST WORDS

If we're not open to correction, we run the risk of becoming inauthentic. The religious leaders of Jesus' day had developed an elaborate system of rituals (masks) that enabled them to appear better on the outside than they really were on the inside. Over time they convinced themselves that they were truly righteous people because they so diligently obeyed all of their man-made rules.

Jesus unleashed his harshest words on them because they professed a high ethic, a worthy set of standards, but didn't put it into practice. He told them, "You are like whitewashed tombs, which look beautiful on the outside but on the inside are full of dead men's bones and everything unclean. In the same way, on the outside you appear to people as righteous but on the inside you are full of hypocrisy and wickedness."[16]

If we're not open to correction, we run the risk of becoming inauthentic.

You've probably noticed that hypocrisy is one of those sins most of us can spot in others without seeing it in ourselves. It's like bad breath. If somebody else has it you want to keep your distance. But nobody can tell if their own breath is sweet or sour.

Take just a moment right now to look at yourself in a mirror. As you gaze at your reflection, ask yourself, "Do I have weaknesses others can see but that I'm refusing to face—weaknesses I pretend are either out of sight or under control? Or am I the kind of person who is comfortable with my strengths and weaknesses and invites others to see them both?"

AN UNEXPECTED TEST

It's a fact of life that you never know when your integrity will be tested. That's a lesson learned by an ambitious nurse who was a candidate to lead the nursing team at a prestigious hospital. The chief of surgery had just completed an operation in which the nurse was assisting when he snapped off his surgical gloves and told her to close the incision.

"But, Doctor, you've only removed eleven sponges. We used twelve."

"I removed them all," the doctor declared. "Now close the incision."

"No!" the nurse objected. "We used twelve sponges and there are only eleven on the table."

"I'll take full responsibility," the surgeon said sternly. "Suture."

"You can't do that," the nurse insisted. "What about the patient?"

The surgeon smiled, lifted his foot, and showed the nurse the twelfth sponge, which he had hidden under his shoe. Smiling, he said, "You'll do. The nursing team is yours to lead."

That nurse passed the integrity test. She held to the highest standard of patient care and put it into practice—even when a much-desired promotion was at stake.

Every day you'll face similar tests. For the most part they'll be unannounced. Some will be subtle, and others will be "in your face." Whether you know it or not, those you lead will be watching you. They'll observe how you handle those unexpected character tests. As you allow the wisdom of Jesus to awaken the leader within you, you *will* grow in integrity. As you do, those you lead will trust you more. As their trust grows, so will their eagerness to follow you.

Of course, integrity alone doesn't make an effective leader. Skilled leaders have to know where they're going. In the next chapter you'll discover how the wisdom of Jesus can enable you to become a visionary leader.

∞

THE WISDOM OF JESUS

- Jesus never wore a mask.

- With Jesus, what you saw was what you got—literally.

- Jesus held to the highest moral ethic and always lived by it.

- Jesus courageously helped people see the gap between their ethic and morality.

- Jesus isn't looking for perfect leaders, but for men and women who hold to a high ethic and want to flesh it out in their lives.

3

LOOK AHEAD

*Y*esterday I was flying from Chicago to West Palm Beach. The pilot had just announced that we were over the city of Orlando when I realized Disney World was 30,000 feet or so below me. A generation ago Walt Disney looked at hundreds of undeveloped acres in southern California and central Florida and saw an imaginary world. Today his dream has become a fun-filled reality that has transformed the entertainment industry. Talk about vision. Here was a man who looked at a swamp—and saw millions of families having fun with a mouse!

But there was a time when Disney was viewed as one thoroughly ordinary man. In fact, he was once fired—get this—because he didn't have any good ideas! How would you like to have been the manager who fired Walt Disney for *that* reason? One thing is certain: Disney had *one* great idea that captured his imagination and made him an internationally recognized leader.

Of course, Disney is just a single example. As I contemplated ordinary people possessing extraordinary vision, a number of well-known leaders came to mind—like the Harvard dropout who started a computer company because he dreamed of creating a personal computer so user-friendly that every person in the country would have one. Today the dream of this man by the name of Bill Gates has changed the world.

Until the night of May 3, 1980, Candy Lightner was perfectly content in her role as a wife and mother. On that tragic night a drunk driver killed her daughter, Cari. Candy's anger over the circumstances that led to her daughter's death prompted her to take action. She began to share a vision of mothers working together to change the way people view drunk driving—a vision that has led to the saving of many lives. Her leadership was instrumental in the formation of Mothers Against Drunk Driving (MADD) and Students Against Drunk Driving (SADD). When asked about the success of MADD, she said, "If you care enough, you can accomplish anything."

It's your dream of the future that will pull you out of bed in the morning and create a current that will draw others toward its realization.

Each of these people was like you and me until the day a compelling vision captured their hearts and minds. Once they locked on to the vision—like a heat-seeking missile—they *had* to pursue their target. They *had* to make it happen—and they *had* to recruit others to help them.

All of your potential to be a man or woman who leads like Jesus will remain like diffused light until a compelling vision focuses it into a laser beam. It's your dream of the future that will pull you out of bed in the morning and create a current that will draw others toward its realization. It's your dream of tomorrow that will cause people to join your church or go to work for your company and give of their time and talents. It's your vision of the future that will give meaning to a committee and purpose to a family.

In this chapter you'll be introduced to four principles that can unleash your potential as a visionary leader.

33

Principle One:

Visionary Leaders Are Shipbuilders, Not Cruise Coordinators

Several years ago my family went on a cruise from Los Angeles to Mexico via Catalina Island. It was our first cruise, and I have to admit I enjoyed every aspect of the experience. The presentation of the food was so impressive I felt like I was destroying a work of art every time I ate. And not only was the food fit for royalty, the entertainment was world-class.

This experience reminded me that I can easily fall into the trap of leading as though I'm a cruise coordinator. In my ministry I cast the vision for an exotic destination ("Let's build a building!"), round up the entertainment ("Bring in the best vocalists and instrumentalists!"), hire a world-class chef ("I'll deliver delicious messages"), and work hard to keep everyone happy ("Let's strengthen the small groups and other support ministries") until we reach our port of call.

I have to constantly remind myself I'm *not* taking our church on a cruise; rather, I'm building a ship. A cruise is a temporary excursion with a point of departure and return—like completing a building project or expanding a company by adding new products or acquiring new divisions. When the project is over the vision has been realized, and everyone is free to go home. A shipbuilder is constructing something that will last for hundreds, if not thousands, of cruises. It's the setting where life is enjoyed and dreams are realized. Visionary leaders build a church made up of people committed to worshiping Jesus, not simply a brick-and-mortar building. They develop a company committed to serving customers instead of merely reaching new sales quotas. They build a family of character rather than just focusing on getting the kids through school.

Jesus' vision wasn't to take his disciples on a luxurious cruise through the Holy Land. He was a shipbuilder. He built a vision into his disciples that has lasted nearly two thousand years and transformed billions of lives. He built a ship that is still sailing. Once you've decided to follow Jesus' example and build a visionary organization that will last for generations, you'll be ready to apply the next three principles of visionary leadership.

Principle Two:

Visionary Leaders Know Their Core Values and Have a Vision That Expresses Them

My middle son, David, is as social as a Labrador retriever. When David was young, isolating him in his room was an effective form of discipline because he hated being alone.

Consequently, I reasoned that this disciplinary technique of isolation should be carved in stone and used in every situation. The first time I tried it on Paul, my youngest son, he smiled. After he had been in his room for several hours, I peeked in and saw him playing on his computer. He liked being alone because it enabled him to do what he enjoyed most.

What I had put to use with my son, David, was a practice, not a value. A practice is an activity or action that may work in one situation but not necessarily in another. Unlike a practice, a value applies to every situation.

Values are also different from principles. A principle is an *external* truth that is as reliable as a physical law such as the law of gravity. When Solomon said, "A gentle answer turns away wrath, but a harsh word stirs up anger,"[1] he stated a principle that is both universal and timeless.

Principles are important because they function like a map allowing us to make wise decisions. If we ignore them or deny their reliability, we become like travelers refusing to use a road map because we don't think it's accurate. While we may acknowledge the reliability of many principles, we only internalize those we deem important. When that happens, the principle has become a value that serves as the *internal* map we use to direct our lives. A value, then, is an internalized principle that guides our decisions.

In fact, every decision we make is driven by a value—it applies to the clothes we wear, the cars we drive, and the food we eat. For instance, a narcissistic principle declares, "If it feels good, do it." This principle asserts that whether or not we do something should be decided by the pleasure it offers.

A value is an internalized principle that guides our decisions.

Several years ago my doctor informed me that my cholesterol was on the high side. As I left his office he handed me a sheet of paper on which was a list of foods I should eat and those I should avoid. On one column was a list of foods I affectionately labeled *Styrofoam*. On the other was a list of my favorites—red meat, bacon, eggs, ham, fried foods, and so on.

My doctor tried to sell me on the principle that says, "Low-fat foods make a healthy body." While I accepted the principle as true, I've had a hard time translating it into a value. In fact, every time I eat a thick, juicy steak I'm acting on the value that says, "If it feels (or, in this case, *tastes*) good, do it."

All of our decisions reveal values. Effective leadership requires identifying those principles that we believe are most important, internalizing them, and allowing them to serve as the map we follow in our decision making.

Identify Your Core Values

While you may have numerous values that influence your life, a *core value* is a tenet you and those you lead have identified as essential and enduring. At your core you're convinced that this value is a key to effective living. The Disney Company has identified "imagination and wholesomeness" as a core value that should be nurtured. The specialty retailer Nordstrom has determined that "taking care of the customer" is a core value that will define and drive their operations. These two companies didn't identify these core values in order to make more money; they've identified them as core values because they believe they are the right way to carry on business.[2] At their core they have a heartfelt belief that these values must be lived out in practice. All of the imagination at the Disney Company and the excellent customer service at Nordstrom are expressions of their core values.

As a leader you can identify your core values and those of the organization you lead by asking yourself, "What is of utmost importance?" "What values are we committed to even if there is no reward for holding to them?" "What values will we still be grasping tightly in twenty or thirty years?" "If I had to explain to someone what I stand for at the core, what would I tell them?"

The Core Values of Jesus

In a sense, when the religious leaders asked Jesus, "Which is the greatest commandment in the Law?"[3] they were asking him to boil down all of the Law into a single core value.

His reply was swift and to the point: "'Love the Lord your God with all your heart and with all your soul and with all your mind.' This is the first and greatest commandment. And the second is like it: 'Love your neighbor as yourself.'"[4]

Every word Jesus spoke, every miracle he performed, and every relationship he cultivated were governed by the core values of love for God and love for neighbor. A love for God compelled him to drive the money changers out of the temple.[5] A love for his neighbor moved him to tears at the grave of Lazarus.[6] That same wondrous, incomprehensible love compelled him to sacrifice his life on a Roman cross outside the city gates of Jerusalem.[7]

Strategies will always have to be adapted to the changes in the world around us. Core values, like biblical principles and values, never change (although they should be regularly evaluated and reaffirmed). That's why it's crucial to identify those timeless values that truly express who you are, those core values that will be embraced by those you lead.

Nobody will buy into your vision just because you tell them to. Remember, leadership is the art of getting others to do what you want them to do because *they* want to do it. People want to do that which expresses *their* own core values. Whether you're leading a family or a company, it's imperative that you get together with your family or team and write out your core values—because your vision will undeniably express those values. Once you've articulated your core values, you'll be ready to apply the next principle.

PRINCIPLE THREE:

VISIONARY LEADERS KNOW THEIR DRIVING PURPOSE AND HAVE A VISION THAT EXPRESSES IT

There is no more important question for a leader to answer than the question, "Why am I here?" Or to put it differently, "Why are we—my family, my business, my ministry, my team—here?" Take a moment right now to see if you have a ready answer. If you can successfully identify your driving purpose, you will be articulating something you will spend the rest of your life pursuing—something around which you can rally those you lead.

Core values, like biblical principles and values, never change.

Mary Kay Ash didn't declare that her company, Mary Kay Cosmetics, exists to provide cosmetics for women and profits for those who sell them. She stated that the purpose for her company is "to give unlimited opportunity to women." Wal-Mart founder Sam Walton didn't invite his employees to join a team that would build the largest retail chain in the world. He proclaimed that they were there "to give ordinary folks the chance to buy the same things as rich people." One of my favorite purpose statements is that of Walt Disney: "To make people happy."[8]

Jesus' Driving Purpose

Not only does our driving purpose give us something to live for, it also gives us something we can look back on as we near the end of our lives and gauge our accomplishments. The night before his death Jesus prayed these words: "Father, ... I have brought you glory on earth by completing the work you gave me to do."[9] Jesus defined that work when he said, "The Son of Man came to seek and to save what was lost."[10] Everything Jesus did was subsumed under that driving purpose.

> *Not only does our driving purpose give us something to live for, it also gives us something we can look back on as we near the end of our lives and gauge our accomplishments.*

As a leader you'll repeatedly encounter forces that will attempt to divert you from your driving purpose. Jesus surely experienced that as well. Yet he never deviated from his mission. At the beginning of his ministry, having been led by the Spirit into the desert, Jesus was presented several strategic opportunities that seemed to promise immediate riches, power, and fame—opportunities that would have utilized his unique abilities.[11] The Bible tells us that Jesus would not be swayed.

If you're a leader you'll undoubtedly face situations in which you're tempted to use your power, prestige, or position to gratify a legitimate appetite in an illegitimate way. The Bible is filled with stories of people who succumbed to that temptation—men like David, Samson, and Solomon. Jesus, on the other hand, refused to be turned aside from his mission. He refused to use his power to indulge any appetites in a way that did not support his purpose.

Make no mistake about it, once you've articulated your driving purpose you'll be bombarded with opportunities that promise to utilize your unique talents and present you with great rewards. Unfortunately, seizing these opportunities will almost always mean forfeiting your purpose. Not only must you identify your driving purpose, you must doggedly pursue it, refusing to allow anything or anyone to turn your energies in another direction. As you stay true to your purpose, you'll be ready to implement the fourth principle.

PRINCIPLE FOUR:

VISIONARY LEADERS HAVE A VIVID BLOW YOUR SOCKS OFF VISION

Several years ago I was privileged to play a leadership role in helping a church acquire one of the most desirable pieces of property in the Portland, Oregon, metropolitan area. When I told my good friend and land developer Bob Bobosky that I thought a particular piece of property would be a great place for a church, he shook his head and said, "There's no way we'll ever be able to acquire *that* piece of property." He paused a moment and continued, "But I'll check it out."

Two years later the church was making plans to build on that location. In the process I realized that this particular ministry would never fully embrace my core values and driving purpose. My destiny was not to serve a more traditional church but to lead in the building of a church that would provide a safe and creative setting for people to grow spiritually—a safe place for my unchurched friends to connect with God.

Several years later when I walked away from the land, the financial resources, and the building plans, Bob said, "I'm really going to miss that property." And I didn't blame him. After all, he had spent an enormous amount of time and energy making the deal that enabled the church to acquire the land.

While I felt emotionally devastated by the loss, I had culti-
40 | vated an even bigger vision. "Bob," I said, "I'm going to tell you something nobody knows but my wife. I never intended the church to remain on that property. It's too small. I figured we'd grow and then relocate."

"And where were you thinking we'd relocate to?" I took a deep breath because I was about to share with one of my closest friends a *Blow Your Socks Off Vision* that had been brewing within me for a couple of years. "Okay, Bob—here's what I've been thinking. For the last two years every time I drive into Portland from the south I pass by a hill on the east of Interstate 5, and I see a church sitting on it. I see thousands of people from all over the city being drawn to it. I see professional men and women who have never been to church learning about how they can have a relationship with Jesus."

Bob interrupted my energetic description. "Exactly where is that hill?"

I gave him the precise location. He paused for so long I thought he had hung up the phone. Finally he said, "You're not going to believe this, Bill. Unknown to anybody else, my wife and I bought that hill thirty days ago."

A tingle rushed down my spine. Thirty minutes later, Bob and his wife were at my house. Fifteen minutes after that we were standing on the summit of that hill, dreaming of what would some day be.

Effective leaders have a compelling *Blow Your Socks Off Vision*. Throughout his career as governor of California and his two terms as president, Ronald Reagan spoke of America as the "shining city on a hill." Leaving the White House in 1980, he said, "I've spoken of the shining city all my political life, but I don't know if I ever quite communicated what I saw when I said it. But in my mind it was a tall, proud city, built on rocks stronger than oceans, windswept, God-blessed, and teeming with people of all kinds living in harmony and peace, a city with free ports that hummed with commerce and creativity, and if there had to be city walls, the walls had doors and the doors were open to anyone with the will and the heart to get in."[12]

Martin Luther King Jr. gave one of the most passionate descriptions of a *Blow Your Socks Off Vision* as he spoke to a huge crowd from the base of the Lincoln Memorial. He said he dreamed of an America where his children would not be judged by the color of their skin, but by their character.

> *Effective leaders have a compelling Blow Your Socks Off Vision.*

41

Howard Schultz, the founder of Starbucks, had a *Blow Your Socks Off Vision* of coffee shops where quality coffee would be served in a comfortable atmosphere.

Our ability to create reveals one key way in which we bear the image of God.

Jesus himself had a *Blow Your Socks Off Vision* of a kingdom where citizens live like their heavenly Father.

What about you? What is your *Blow Your Socks Off Vision*? If it's something that has captured your soul, then state it as descriptively as you can—and by all means share it with those you lead. If you aren't sure what it is, then read on.

Finding Your Blow Your Socks Off Vision

The ability to dream big comes from a creative element God instilled in every man, woman, and child. The Bible tells us that God made man in his own image. In fact, within the span of two verses we're told four times that God made man in his image.[13] I'm convinced our ability to create reveals one key way in which we bear the image of God. He is the master builder, the great visionary who sees the end from the beginning. Creating us in his image is the cause, and our desire to create and build is the effect.

Your *Blow Your Socks Off Vision* will flow from your imagination and be fueled by your past experiences and present prayers (in later chapters we'll examine in more detail the role of prayer). Turning your imagination loose may take some practice (we'll look at this in more detail in chapter 12). You may be so afraid of failure that you dare to dream only within very specific and restrictive boundaries. You may be reluctant to set the bar too high for fear that you couldn't possibly jump over it. Yet, if truth be told, a *Blow Your Socks Off Vision* knows no boundaries. It has massive resources at its disposal. It's a dream that can be ten, twenty, thirty, or more years in the future.

Ask yourself this question: "If money and other resources were not an issue, what would my future, or that of my organization, look like?" Challenge your leadership team to develop a *Blow Your Socks Off Vision* for their particular area of responsibility and for the entire organization. Encourage them to describe their *Blow Your Socks Off Vision* as vividly and descriptively as possible.

Jesus' Blow Your Socks Off Vision

Visionary leaders are like the child who feverishly worked on a drawing during his kindergarten class. Curious as to what had so captured the child's attention, the teacher approached his desk, leaned over, and gazed at the image on the paper. "What are you drawing?" the teacher asked.

"A picture of God," the boy said without looking up.

The teacher smiled. "But, sweetheart, nobody knows what God looks like."

"I know," he said. "But they will when I'm done."

Visionary leaders see the invisible so clearly that when they're finished "drawing" it or describing it, those they lead can see it too. As Jonathan Swift once said, they've mastered "the art of seeing the invisible."[14]

Jesus repeatedly painted a verbal picture of the future God was preparing for his followers. He described a day when they would live in his presence and have a room in the home of heaven's King.[15] He promised there would be a renewal of all creation, and his followers would rule with him in his kingdom.[16] Jesus spoke in great detail about the attitudes of those who would live in his future kingdom. He said the first would be last;[17] the humble would be lifted up;[18] and the hungry would be satisfied.[19] Talk about vision!

> *Ultimately, our drive, our passion, to be visionary leaders should flow from a desire to emulate Jesus.*

The future Jesus described was so compelling that it has captured the imagination of men and women for nearly two thousand years. Ultimately, our drive, our passion, to be visionary leaders should flow from a desire to emulate Jesus—the greatest leader of all time.

43

THE WISDOM OF JESUS

- Jesus knew his core values, and they governed all he did.

- Jesus knew his driving purpose and lived to accomplish it.

- Jesus didn't allow anything or anyone to divert him from his purpose.

- Jesus never used his unique abilities for self-serving purposes.

- Jesus had a *Blow Your Socks Off Vision* of the future and eagerly shared it with his team.

4

LEAD THE CHARGE

I recently read that a locomotive on the run can crash through a five-foot-thick steel-reinforced concrete wall. I can't imagine who would build such a wall across a railroad track. Even harder to imagine is why somebody would park a car or truck where it could be hit by a train. But just last year a man in Oregon parked his pickup in the middle of a railroad crossing while he talked on his cell phone. I suspect you can already see what's coming. Unfortunately, he didn't—and the train slammed into his pickup at 55 miles an hour and pushed it for about a half a mile before the truck slipped off the side of the track. Authorities figured he was so engrossed in the phone conversation that he didn't hear the whistle of the approaching train.

While neither a steel-enforced concrete wall nor a pickup truck can slow down a train, its initial movement can be prevented by something much smaller. In fact, a one-inch block of wood lodged in front of each of the mechanical behemoth's wheels will keep it from moving.

Companies, churches, and other organizations also have the power to blast through seemingly insurmountable barriers once they have momentum. Your job as a leader is to empower your organization to achieve that kind of momentum. But like a train, you and those you lead can be stopped before you get moving by something as small as a four-letter word: F-E-A-R.

Fear is an emotion we're all acquainted with. Occasionally a friend or associate may tell us that the fear we feel is only our imagination. "There's nothing to be afraid of," they say confidently. We may listen to their words, grit our teeth, and pretend that they're right. But what we feel is very real indeed. It taunts us. It squeezes our stomach and makes our heart race. It keeps us awake at night. It clouds our mind and creates uncertainty. And often, instead of leading a charge, we're trying to figure out how to limit our losses.

Courage isn't the absence of fear; it's the ability to face our fears and lead effectively in spite of them.

Because fear has the potential to undermine your efforts as a leader, it's essential you learn how to cultivate the courage needed to master it. Please note I said "master" it. I didn't say "eliminate" it. Courage isn't the absence of fear; it's the ability to face our fears and lead effectively in spite of them. Time and again Jesus faced situations that required courage. He didn't back down when challenged by powerful leaders who opposed his cause. He didn't dilute his message when crowds of people stopped following him because his words were too hard. He didn't lie when doing so could have saved his life. Because Jesus led with courage, we can find in his words and in his actions principles that will equip us to lead the charge in the face of fear-provoking circumstances.

COURAGEOUS LEADERS FOCUS ON THEIR PURPOSE, NOT THEIR FEARS

When South Hills Community Church came into existence, it was clear that we had to find a gifted musician to lead our music ministry. I didn't have anybody in mind when a friend called and said he wanted the job. John had served in a number of large churches, and he already had five musicians and several vocalists on his team. There were few musicians in Portland with his credentials and talent.

In spite of John's assets, I had a single concern: Would his style of music support the driving purpose of the church? You see, our purpose was to build a safe and creative setting for people to grow in their relationship with God. John's personal and musical tastes were traditional and formal. He fit perfectly in a large church with a more traditional philosophy and concept of ministry—but would he fit into what we were doing?

I agonized over this decision because I feared we wouldn't find someone with his level of skill and experience. Furthermore, we were friends, and I didn't want to do anything to hurt him. Eventually, however, I allowed the driving purpose of the church to guide my choice, and I turned down his offer.

I'm convinced most of the tough decisions leaders have to make are avoided, not because they don't know *what* to do, but because they're afraid of the consequences. They fear opponents may start a mutiny or abandon ship. You can't allow political pressures to dictate the choices you make as a leader. Once you do, you've become a weather vane, controlled by your environment, rather than a compass that points in the right direction. Instead of focusing on what you fear, concentrate on your driving purpose and core values. These two components are like the banks of a river between which resources are channeled toward the *Blow Your Socks Off Vision*. If you know that a decision supports your core values and driving purpose and will help you accomplish your *Blow Your Socks Off Vision*, then you must have the courage to make it, even if you fear the consequences of doing so.

Keep First Things First

Jesus spent significant time helping his disciples develop the courage to overcome their fears. On one occasion he gave them a simple and straightforward command aimed at busting apart their worry and fear. He said, "But seek first his kingdom and his righteousness, and all these things will be given to you as well."[1]

Pause for just a moment now, and read the next sentence slowly—for it is crucial. *Fear is dispelled when you focus on your purpose.* When everything else is said and done, nothing helps us cultivate courage more effectively than focusing on our driving purpose. It's the key, I believe, to understanding what Jesus meant when he said, "Seek first his kingdom and

Fear is dispelled when you focus on your purpose.

his righteousness." If he had expanded his remarks he might have said, "Keep your life focused on why you're here. As long as you're heading in the right direction, God will take care of the things you fear."

The fundamental truth that fear is dispelled when you focus on your purpose can be applied to the organization you're leading—whether it's your family, business, or church. The next time you're filled with worry over an important decision, ask yourself two questions: First, "Does this course of action support the driving purpose of my life and of the organization I'm leading?" Second, "Does it express our core values?" If it doesn't, toss it aside. If it does, and you've concluded that it's the best possible course of action, then carry it out with courage.

Unfortunately, there will be occasions when you'll be operating within the banks of your driving purpose and core values—and you will still wrestle with fear. Uncertainty may cloud your thinking. On those occasions you'll do well to apply the next principle.

Courageous Leaders Know That Failure Is the Seed of Success

I'll never forget the words of Dr. Howard Hendricks, or "Prof" as we students affectionately called him. "Gentlemen," he barked, with his right hand jammed into his pants pocket. "Never forget, when it comes to good ideas, quantity always brings quality!" What Dr. Hendricks was telling us was that we shouldn't be afraid of coming up with "bad" ideas, because it takes hundreds of bad ideas to come up with a single, fantastic, unbelievable, hit-it-out-of-the-ballpark idea.

Building on that concept let me offer what I call the *law of success*, which simply says, "Failure is the seed of success."

Of course, I realize most of us have heard some variation on that idea time and again. The problem is most of us have never embraced it. We think this little maxim is simply a way of coping with disappointment . . . a pep talk after a losing effort . . . an emotional anesthetic. But it's not. It's a fact of life. Failure isn't the back door to success—it's the front door.

When I moved to Oregon seventeen years ago I came with an impressive list of ministry successes. The Young Life club I led while in seminary had exploded with growth. We saw so many kids become believers in Jesus that we ended up starting a church in our apartment—a church that grew so fast we were able to hire a pastor before six months had passed. During my last two years of seminary I traveled around the country speaking to various high school groups. Following graduation I moved to Houston, where the first church I served as pastor grew by forty percent a year. When we completed a building project after two years and immediately went to two morning services, several people suggested I lead church growth seminars.

> *The law of success simply says, "Failure is the seed of success."*

The success I experienced in Texas followed me to Oregon. Four years after I arrived in Portland, the church I served more than tripled in size, acquired a multimillion-dollar piece of land on a strategic intersection, and raised substantial funds for a new building.

During my sixth year in Portland a large congregation in the San Francisco Bay area wanted me to move to California and lead their church—an offer I declined. Their only concern was that I had never experienced failure.

Sounds pretty impressive, doesn't it? I seemed to be having ministry success without the pain of failure. Of course, I had had my share of struggles—but nothing too serious. Yet all that was to change on the day I was taken aback by a vote of "no confidence" from our board of elders, who asked me point-blank, "What do you intend to do?"

Unless a kernel of wheat falls to the ground and dies, it remains only a single seed. But if it dies, it produces many seeds.

Failure stared me in the face, and fear wrapped its fingers around my throat and squeezed. Determined to model how to lose with grace, I walked away from a vision I had carefully cultivated for nine years. I turned my back on millions of dollars' worth of resources.

The overwhelming sense of failure felt like a knife in my heart that someone with cruel intent was twisting and turning unceasingly. I remember being told, "The day will come when you'll look back on this as one of the best things that ever happened to you."

"Right!" I said with a look as sincere as a mannequin's smile. I believed that this experience would be about as good for me as the Battle of the Little Bighorn had been for Gen. George Custer.

That was nine years ago. Today I would have to say that the greatest lesson I've learned from that experience was this: *Failure is the seed of success.*

Listen to what Jesus said in reference to his impending death: "I tell you the truth, unless a kernel of wheat falls to the ground and dies, it remains only a single seed. But if it dies, it produces many seeds."[2] Jesus' enemies heralded his death as the end of a small and pesky religious movement. They believed that by killing Jesus they would silence him.

Following the Lord's death the disciples were left reeling by the sense that just maybe they had wasted over three years of their lives. Everything they had hoped for was gone. Everything they had prepared for was gone. Everything they had invested in was gone. Jesus—their master, their teacher, their friend—had died, and they were all failures, both in their own eyes and in the eyes of almost everyone else.

They were so blind to the law of success that even when they heard that Jesus had risen from the dead, some of them doubted. I don't blame them. Yet when they finally saw the risen Lord, everything changed. The seed that had died and been buried had come to life and would produce many more seeds.

Of course, I realize Jesus *was* talking about his own death and resurrection. But he was also stating a principle of life that his death and resurrection validated—one that bears on your current situation as well: *Failure is the seed of success.* If you will but embrace that reality, you'll discover it's a limitless source of courage.

> *Once we accept the fact that failure happens, we can courageously face failure because we know it can't be completely avoided.*

Does the law of success mean we should seek failure? Of course not! Does it mean failure is okay? By no means! It simply means we don't need to fear failure, because it cannot defeat us in the end. I'm reminded of the extraordinary words of M. Scott Peck that appear in the first line of his best-selling book, *The Road Less Traveled:*

> Life is difficult. This is a great truth, one of the greatest truths. It is a great truth because once we truly see this truth, we transcend it. Once we truly know that life is difficult—once we truly understand it and accept it—then life is no longer difficult. Because once it is accepted, the fact that life is difficult no longer matters.[3]

Failure is an inevitable part of life. When we embrace that truth, we transcend it. Once we accept the fact that failure happens, we can courageously face failure because we know it can't be completely avoided. Instead of making leadership decisions that keep us from losing, we can make decisions we think will advance our cause. And when we fail, the lessons we'll learn will enable us to succeed later on.

All you have to do is think of the great championship football teams of past years to know what I'm saying is true. Denver, Green Bay, San Francisco, Dallas—and others—all lost big games before they ever won THE BIG ONE. The same is true of basketball teams. The Chicago Bulls repeatedly lost play-off games before they finally put together one of the greatest teams in National Basketball Association history.

Courage has no greater ally than preparation—and fear has no greater enemy.

I hate to lose. I wish I never again had to experience the pain of losing. But as much as I hate losing, I do realize God has ordered the universe in such a way that losing is the seed of success. Once you grasp that truth, your view of challenges will be transformed. Instead of being afraid that you'll strike out when you step up to the plate, you'll concentrate on staying true to form and making contact with the ball. If you do, you'll get your share of base hits and even home runs. Rather than trying to keep from losing, you'll be able to concentrate on leading the charge. Your fear of failure will be eclipsed by your passion to bring into reality the *Blow Your Socks Off Vision* that has captured your heart.

COURAGEOUS LEADERS OVERCOME FEAR WITH PREPARATION

Courage has no greater ally than preparation—and fear has no greater enemy. The great basketball coach Pat Riley summed it up when he wrote, "Being ready isn't enough, you have to be prepared. . . . Preparation demands mental and physical conditioning and conscious planning. A player who is just ready and not totally prepared simply increases risk."[4]

Jesus not only understood the importance of this courage builder, he put it into practice as he equipped the disciples for ministry. Jesus didn't wait until the birth of the church and then hope against hope that his team would be able to get the job done. He *prepared* his early followers to lead the church forward in the great mission of spreading the good news about Jesus.

Scrimmage!

On one occasion Jesus sent his followers to surrounding villages so they could practice declaring the message. Rather than only directing them to friendly towns, he sent them to hostile villages as well. He told them where to go, what to say, and how to respond to both acceptance and rejection.[5] He let his team scrimmage in preparation for what would happen after his departure.

When the disciples returned, Jesus took them right back to the practice field. This time he asked them to feed five thousand men with two fish and five loaves of bread.[6] Jesus took what they had, miraculously divided it, and fed the masses.

It's easy when reading the story to be impressed with the miracle. But what we don't want to miss is how Jesus used the feeding of the five thousand to prepare his disciples for seemingly impossible situations they would face in the future. After his departure they would find themselves leading others into places where their resources would surely be inadequate. At such times they could either allow fear to hold them back—or they could remember the day Jesus prepared them for such a challenge by taking what they had and using it to feed the masses.

As leaders we need to place a high value on preparation. Former Miami Dolphins coach Don Shula noted that every National Football League coach begins every season by calling the team together and outlining the goals he hopes they will accomplish. It's no surprise that every coach says basically the same thing: We want to make the play-offs and win the Super Bowl.

So what's the difference between coaches who build a championship team and those who don't? Shula remarked, "What's more important than these goals is the follow-up—the attention to detail, demand for practice perfection, and all the things that separate the teams that win from the teams that don't."[7]

I'm convinced a major factor that sets courageous leaders apart is their preparation. Because they've taken the time to prepare for important decisions, they can confidently lead the charge. The next time you feel your courage draining away as you face an important challenge, ask yourself, "Are there steps I can take to be better prepared?" But, as you'll soon see, no preparation is more important than spiritual preparation.

COURAGEOUS LEADERS ARE AWARE OF GOD'S PRESENCE

When I was in the ninth grade, Ron Kompton despised me. A fellow student, Ron looked like a giant and stood as a man among boys. He was six feet three inches tall and weighed 230 pounds. I was only five feet nine inches tall and weighed 130 pounds. Ron's fist was almost as large as my head.

One night Ron arrived late at a party. When he discovered I was there, he hunted me down. In a matter of minutes he was calling me names and shoving me around. Like an idiot I allowed him to coax me into the front yard where he said he was going to kill me.

I did everything short of falling on my knees and crying like a baby to talk Ron out of beating me to a pulp—and I would have done that if I had thought it would save me.

We were standing in the yard surrounded by about thirty kids who were urging us to get it on when suddenly a car screeched to a halt at the curb. A moment later the door slammed and someone yelled out, "Kompton!"

I recognized the voice. It was my best friend, Mike Temple. Mike was the only guy in town bigger and meaner than Ron Kompton. Before graduating from high school, Mike made the all-state football team twice as a fullback. Later he played college ball for Oklahoma State University. He was a tough kid, and he loved to fight.

Mike pushed his way through the crowd, stomped up to Kompton, shoved him back, and said, "Kompton, if you're going to touch Perkins, you'll have to go through me!"

I felt a surge of courage and stepped up to Ron. "That's right, Kompton," I said. "And don't you ever forget it!"

Ron started whimpering about how he didn't realize Mike and I were buddies. He assured my friend he'd never bother me again—and he didn't.[8]

I like to tell that story because it illustrates how Jesus fights for us. No leader who has a relationship with him will ever be alone. He'll always be there when we need him. Just as Mike's presence dispelled my fear and infused me with courage, so an awareness of God's presence brings rock-solid confidence.

The night before his death Jesus met with his disciples in a secluded room in downtown Jerusalem. Aware that they would soon be on their own, he made a promise aimed at busting their fear and bolstering their courage. Jesus said, "I will not leave you as orphans; I will come to you."[9]

> *No leader who has a relationship with Jesus will ever be alone. He'll always be there when we need him.*

Throughout the Bible God bolstered the confidence of fearful leaders with the promise of his presence. When Moses expressed reluctance to lead the Hebrew people to freedom, God said, "I will be with you."[10] A generation later, when Joshua took the mantle of leadership, he stood alone. Moses was gone, as were most of his friends. Joshua was an old man facing the challenge of driving the more adequately armed Canaanites from their fortified cities. When God saw this frightened servant, he didn't remind Joshua of the years of preparation he had just gone through in the desert. Instead, God emphatically and repeatedly assured Joshua of his courage-building, never-failing presence.[11]

Of course, our faith in God must be developed. And in the next chapter you'll want to look for insights from the wisdom of Jesus that will show you how your dependence on God can transform you personally and as a leader. But let me first conclude this chapter with a story that illustrates the importance of courage.

STONEWALL JACKSON'S APPRAISAL

During the Civil War, Gen. Thomas "Stonewall" Jackson reprimanded Gen. Richard Ewell for a strategic error made during a battle. Impressed with the courage of a cavalry officer who displayed conspicuous gallantry in rallying the Federal troops on the field of battle, General Ewell had ordered his soldiers not to shoot at the man. Jackson reproved his subordinate by remarking shrewdly, "Shoot the brave officers and the cowards will run away and take their men with them!"[12]

Jackson had it right, didn't he? Courageous leaders empower their troops to accomplish what fear would keep them from doing. Your own courage as a leader is crucial to the success of the team you lead. With that truth in mind—raise the flag, and lead the charge!

∞

THE WISDOM OF JESUS

- Jesus always focused on his purpose, not on the dangers he might encounter.

- Jesus always kept first things first.

- Jesus believed that failure is the seed of success.

- Jesus prepared himself and those he led for the challenges they would face.

- Jesus lived with a conscious awareness of his Father's presence.

5

DEPEND ON GOD

When you place your faith in someone or something, you unleash power on your behalf. Every mechanical device at your fingertips is powerless until you turn it on and trust it to do whatever it was created to do. The power of a passenger plane does you no good until you trust it to carry you from one place to another. Friends and physicians, coaches and teachers are all powerless to help you until you trust them.

Faith is such an integral part of your life that there isn't a waking moment when you're not exercising it. When your alarm goes off in the morning and you hit the snooze button, you trust that the button will turn off the music and that it will come back on again in ten minutes. On your way to work you trust drivers of oncoming cars, whom you don't know, to stay in their lane of traffic. At work you trust elevators, computers, colleagues, and friends. At lunch and dinner you eat food you believe is nourishing—or at the very least nontoxic. When you walk in the door of your home and flip a light switch, you believe the light will come on. When you finally climb into bed at the end of the day, you trust the smoke detector in the hall to alert you and your family to a fire should one break out while you are sleeping.

Every moment of every day you're exercising faith in something or someone—and then reaping the benefits. In fact, most of the time you do it without a moment's hesitation. And just as you freely trust all sorts of things throughout the day, so Jesus trusted his heavenly Father. And his faith gave him an unbroken connection with God's power.

Throughout the course of his earthly ministry Jesus told his disciples to trust in God and also showed them how to do it. From Jesus' perspective, his followers' faith in God would be the single most important leadership quality they would possess. Jesus wanted them to be leaders whose faith in God made them conduits of his power. And when they did trust in God, amazing things happened to them and to those they led.

When you place your faith in someone or something, you unleash power on your behalf.

I'd love to trade places with the disciples for just a day and see Jesus firsthand. What would it be like to talk with someone who trusted God *all* the time? What would it be like to watch someone whose faith was undiluted by doubt? And perhaps more important, what would I learn from Jesus that would awaken my own faith in God and transform me as a leader?

I realize because Jesus was the Son of God he possessed full deity. In that respect I am unlike him. But he was also *fully* human. He ate, drank, and slept like any other human being. He experienced joy, grief, anger, and love. He had a normal male sex drive and found women attractive. He was well acquainted with power and the temptation to abuse it. Jesus dealt with a busy schedule, a demanding team, and lofty goals, as well as physical and emotional exhaustion.

In the face of the same kinds of pressures you encounter as a leader, Jesus always trusted in God and tapped into his power. In his humanity he related to God, his heavenly Father, exactly as you should. He never stopped trusting in God and carrying out his will.

And by example Jesus showed us how we too can be leaders of faith. As I've examined his life, I've discovered five practices we can surely apply to our lives. I'm convinced that these five characteristics must be reproduced in a leader who truly desires to possess the kind of faith that taps into the power of God.

FAITH BUILDER NUMBER ONE:

KEEP IN TOUCH WITH GOD

The Devil's Greatest Tool

Several years ago I ran across a short poem by Gloria Pitzer that expresses a problem every leader faces. She wrote:

Procrastination is my sin,

It brings me naught but sorrow.

I know that I should stop it.

In fact I will ... tomorrow.

There are few things easier to do than to put off until tomorrow something that should be done today. According to popular legend the devil once called a conference with his most sinister cohorts. The purpose of the meeting was to come up with a lie they could use to keep people from taking God seriously. One demon lifted a gnarled finger and said, "I have it! We could tell them there is no heaven."

The devil shook his head from side to side and said, "That won't work. There are too many people who already believe in heaven."

No sooner had those words left his mouth than another demon blurted out, "Then let's tell them there is no hell."

Again the devil turned down the suggestion, insisting that too many people had tasted the pain of hell on earth to believe such a lie.

Finally a third demon smiled and said, "I think I've got just the lie. We'll tell them there is no hurry."

The devil leaped to his feet and exclaimed, "Perfect! *Everyone* will believe that."

Tomorrow Never Comes

For some reason that legend has a spooky ring of truth to it. I know there are many times when I fall for that line. And what concerns me most is that it's my relationship with God where I'm most vulnerable. The relationship that was the most important to Jesus, and should be to me as well, usually isn't. I find it awfully easy to put off until "later" a private meeting with God. Unfortunately, "later" is always just that—"later." It's like the sign I saw on a furniture store in Santa Fe, New Mexico. The faded paint told me the sign had been there a long time. It read: "Tomorrow we will give away everything in the store." For a moment I was excited, and then I realized the sign would say the same thing the next day, and the next, and the next. By putting off the big "giveaway" until tomorrow, it would never take place.

I know I'm not the only leader who struggles with spiritual procrastination. For years I've had a weekly meeting with a group of business leaders—and they all have the same struggle. Initially when I looked at the example of Jesus I discovered some impressive truths. Mark made this observation: "Very early in the morning, while it was still dark, Jesus got up, left the house and went off to a solitary place, where he prayed."[1]

Later, Mark described another situation where, at the end of a busy day, Jesus sent the disciples off in a boat and then "went up on a mountainside to pray."[2] It was Luke who thought it important to mention that Jesus prayed all night before he selected the twelve disciples.[3] The crucial point is this: *Jesus spent an entire night in prayer while making an important leadership decision.*

I'm sure you're getting the drift—Jesus never put off his appointment with the heavenly Father. Nothing crowded out that meeting. Nothing! Not family, friends, teammates, sick people, important decisions, or impending disasters. The greatest leader of all time made a daily meeting with God his top priority. The bottom line is this: The more time you spend with God the better you'll know him; the better you know him the more you'll trust him; the more you trust him the more you'll tap into his power.

A Crucial Insight

Realizing this truth doesn't solve my problem. As I come to acknowledge this truth, it frustrates me, because I don't want to meet with God because I *should*. More than fulfilling an obligation, I want to share Jesus' thinking and motivation. Occasionally I'll sense I've got it—like a passing insight into a complicated math problem—and then it slips away. Realizing that Jesus had daily meetings with his Father shows me *what* I should do. But I'm convinced the key to making those meetings a priority rests in understanding *why* Jesus valued them. And so, having seen that a daily meeting with God is important, let's take the next step and examine just what it is that characterized Jesus' meetings with the Father. I trust you'll discover principles that will motivate you to make daily contact with God a priority so your faith can be strengthened.

> *The more time you spend with God the better you'll know him; the better you know him the more you'll trust him; the more you trust him the more you'll tap into his power.*

FAITH BUILDER NUMBER TWO:

FACE YOUR FEARS WITH GOD

Most leaders allow their followers to see only their public face. What happens behind closed doors is strictly off-limits. Not so with Jesus. He allowed his disciples to observe him during his moments of greatest vulnerability. The clearest example occurred on the night before his death. Following the completion of the Passover meal, eleven of the disciples—Judas had already left—walked with Jesus to a garden on the summit of a small hill just beyond the walls of Jerusalem. At the gate of the garden Jesus asked his closest friends—Peter, James, and John—to continue on with him. The rest of the disciples found a comfortable place to rest and fell asleep by the gate.

After they had walked a short way Jesus told the three that he would continue on alone a little farther. But first he told them something they had never heard him say before. He said he was so overwhelmed with sorrow that he was on the verge of death.[4] For the first time since they had come to know him, Jesus was visibly depressed.

I've never met a leader who hasn't faced a challenge so great that he or she felt as overwhelmed as someone trying to push an elephant up a flight of stairs. On those occasions depression and despair become unwanted companions.

Jesus' Darkest Night

When Jesus entered the garden that night the reality of what was about to happen must have felt like a sucker punch to the stomach and a hard right to the chin. He staggered and fell to the ground.[5] With his face pressed against the dirt of the garden, he agonized in prayer.

In Hebrews 5:7–10 the author describes what the disciples heard as Jesus talked with his Father. When I read this passage, I feel uncomfortable because it seems as though I've come upon someone in a very private and personal moment. It's almost like passing by an open window and hearing a man sobbing aloud. Instead of moving on, I linger and listen as he laments a broken romance or failed business or death of a loved one.

But Jesus actually invited his disciples into the garden so they could hear his prayer and record it for us. Matthew tells us what he said,[6] and the author of Hebrews tells us how he said it.[7] Jesus pleaded with God three times to let the cup of death pass him by; he pleaded with "loud cries and tears."[8] So intense was his distress that "his sweat was like drops of blood"[9]—indicating such emotional turmoil that the small capillaries under the surface of his skin ruptured, causing blood to ooze out along with his sweat.

The Real Battle

Had I sat with the disciples and been aware of what would happen the next day, I would have concluded Jesus wasn't up to the task. If just the *thought* of the crucifixion affected him so dramatically, what would the actual event itself do to him? But that's the difference between Jesus and the rest of us. For Jesus the battle occurred in the garden. It was there he experienced the depths of agony.

Once Jesus climbed to his feet and left the garden, he never looked back. He endured betrayal, rejection, beatings, humiliation, and injustice—all before the hours spent hanging on the cross. At the place of execution, nails were driven into his wrists and feet and he was suspended between the gray Judean sky and the blood-soaked earth. So galvanized was his faith that throughout the entire ordeal he continually trusted in his Father and expressed compassion and concern for those around him.

I'm convinced the key to such confidence rests in Gethsemane. You and I might pray when we face a crisis—but do we walk away from that prayer with a supernatural confidence? I hope so. Are we then able to lead the charge with equal courage? I hope so. But to be perfectly honest, I'm not batting a thousand on that one. Sometimes I get so consumed in my desire to meet with associates and strategize about how to solve the problem that I haven't got time to pray—or I don't take the time to pray. While such planning is crucial, when it crowds out my time with God, I have, according to the trite adage, "put the cart before the horse."

My priorities are disordered in the face of a crisis because they are disordered *before* the crisis. The place to face my fears is with God. If I make spending time with him a daily habit, then I'll discover he can be trusted because he helps me overcome my daily doubts and fears. If I can trust him with my

63

routine struggles, then I'll be able to confidently approach him in faith when a big crisis hits.

Keep This Key

A story is told about a widow who while cleaning out her husband's belongings discovered dozens of keys she couldn't identify. Were they relics from worthless projects long forgotten? Or were they claims to important treasure? How would she ever find out? After exhausting all suggestions, the best she could do was admonish readers of a national newspaper column to take better care of important keys—disposing of worthless ones and specially marking those of value.

> *In our search for the key to a bold faith in God, we need to hold on to the one marked: Face Your Fears with God.*

In our search for the key to a bold faith in God, we need to hold on to the one marked: *Face Your Fears with God.* When you find it, and use it every day, you'll discover that it opens doors of confidence you never thought possible. But there's a third key, or faith builder, that's of equal importance.

FAITH BUILDER NUMBER THREE:

BE AUTHENTIC WITH GOD

I can think of a couple of reasons why we isolate ourselves from others. Our culture admires independent tough guys like Dirty Harry, Rambo, Terminator, Robocop, and James Bond. In recent years women on the big screen have become as tough as the men. Nobody gives an inch. Nobody opens up. Nobody gets hurt. Yet, while we may be respected for an indifferent and tough facade, it does not lead to intimacy—but it does protect us from rejection. Nobody wants to disclose their real fears and true feelings to a friend and have them walk away.

And of course as leaders we're always told to keep our cards close to the vest. If we reveal our true thoughts, it might give an advantage to the competition. Nobody wants to do that!

Hide-and-seek

Ultimately, such hiding does more damage than good. In *The Transparent Self*, psychologist Sidney Jourard shares the results of illuminating studies on the topic of self-disclosure. His most important finding is that the human personality has a natural inclination to reveal itself. Furthermore, when that inclination is blocked and we close ourselves to others, it is very likely that we will experience emotional difficulties.[10]

What fascinates me is that we not only hide from each other, but we also hide from God. We talk to him as though he's supposed to be impressed with the tough-guy act. We're so afraid of rejection that we try to conceal ourselves from the One who already knows everything about us. By hiding from God we reveal that we don't trust him to accept us where we are and to help us move forward in the process of becoming better leaders. Such a fear of rejection is a powerful impediment to faith.

We're so afraid of rejection that we try to conceal ourselves from the One who already knows everything about us.

Jesus would have nothing to do with hiding. He didn't play games when he met with God. He made it clear that he desperately wanted to avoid being nailed to a cross. He didn't hide the fact that he didn't want to experience isolation from his Father. He expressed his feelings with loud crying and tears.

Once more I'm compelled to peel away the obvious and look for something more. I want to know what enabled Jesus to be so authentic when he met with his Father. The personal change we long for will only occur as we alter our thinking and motivation. Acknowledging that truth, let's consider why Jesus felt free to be authentic when he met with his Father.

FAITH BUILDER NUMBER FOUR:

REALIZE YOU'VE GOT NOTHING TO HIDE

Few things get leaders into trouble more quickly than an unwillingness to admit their shortcomings and sins. President Nixon might have saved his presidency if he had immediately admitted his role in the Watergate crimes. Instead, he frantically tried to cover his tracks. Ultimately, it was the cover-up that forced his resignation.

Had President Clinton told the truth when first asked about Monica Lewinsky, he undoubtedly could have spared himself a humiliating and protracted ordeal.

Time and again leaders slip into a pattern of cover-up and denial. Because Jesus knew that his Father had seen it all, he knew he had nothing to hide.

Of course, it's not really that simple—because Jesus never sinned. He, in fact, had no sins to cover up. However, he did not always have what we might call "positive" emotions. He could have chosen to hide emotions of frustration, weariness, loneliness, anger, and the like; he could have just kept them inside and not expressed them to the One who sent him to earth.

Yet we see Jesus begging his Father to let the cup of death pass him by.[11] He made no effort to conceal his natural human resistance to the Father's plan. Why? In part because he knew full well that his Father could see his thoughts and feelings. Why try to hide something that's already in plain view? It would be as futile as trying to hide the sun on a clear day. We may try to conceal our feelings from God, but those feelings don't go away. Instead they become like a loaded gun waiting for a crisis to pull the trigger.

66

The Cover-up

Sometimes our efforts to cover up are sophisticated and hard to spot. In fact, we ourselves may not even be completely aware of what we're doing. There may be times when a leader will try to conceal his or her misdeeds by minimizing them. "It wasn't that big a deal," he'll say about an inappropriate use of funds or an abuse of power. "Don't sweat it," she'll plead. "It only involved a few dollars."

The more we open up and show God what we're really like on the inside, the more we'll discover that he can be trusted with the truth about us.

Or she'll justify what she's done. "Under the circumstances it *was* the right thing to do," she'll insist. "If I hadn't done it first, somebody else would have."

We've become experts at looking at our fears and failures through the wrong end of a microscope. I know I do. But it's a waste of time to try to pull such tricks on God.

Because we generally don't trust other people, we've become so skilled at shielding ourselves that it's hard to switch gears and deal authentically with God. The only way to overcome the tendency to hide from God is by meeting with him daily—with a firm commitment to be transparent. The more we open up and show God what we're really like on the inside, the more we'll discover that he *can* be trusted with the truth about us.

FAITH BUILDER NUMBER FIVE:

REALIZE THAT YOU'VE GOT NOTHING TO LOSE

Yet we may find, as we open up with God and speak authentically, that something else may hinder our spiritual progress. Occasionally I'll talk with leaders who have a superstitious view of God. They're reluctant to hand over their valuables because they're afraid he'll keep them. In an act of self-protection and self-sufficiency, they cling to their secrets, their fears, their hopes, and their dreams. Somehow they think that to clutch their valuables will protect them.

Jesus had no such misconceptions. That's why he told his Father three times, "Yet not as I will, but as you will."[12] Jesus willingly opened his hand and offered his Father his most valuable possession—his life. While God's will often goes against the grain of our personal wishes, it's never second best. No one who gives God their prized possessions will later regret it.

One Determined Boy

I'm reminded of the story of the four-year-old boy who slid his hand into a valuable vase and then couldn't get it out. His mother calmed his fears but couldn't free his hand. She pulled on the vase without success. She squirted liquid soap over his hand and still couldn't get the hand to slip through the narrow neck of the vase. Finally she gave up and told the boy, "Your dad will be home in a little while. I'm sure he can get your hand out."

A plate of warm cookies and a glass of cold milk helped get the boy's mind off his predicament. But nothing could keep his mother from worrying about the vase. She knew they could break it, but it was an heirloom that had been in her family for generations. When her husband finally walked into the house, a teary-eyed boy and a distraught wife greeted him. After a few minutes of struggle he declared, "I'll have to break the vase."

Using a tiny hammer he lightly tapped on the body of the priceless heirloom. The porcelain cracked and fell apart, revealing the boy's clutched fist.

Surprised, the two adults looked at each other. "Have you been clutching your fist while we were trying to get your hand out of the vase?" his father asked.

The child nodded his head as tears flowed from his eyes.

His mother placed a hand on the boy's shoulder and asked, "Now, why would you do that?"

"Because I didn't want to let go of my quarter," he said, as he opened his hand and uncovered a shiny quarter.

Because he refused to open his hand and let go of the quarter, the boy destroyed a family heirloom. The same thing happens to us when we refuse to open our hands for God. When

Jesus said, "Not as I will, but as you will," he was opening his hands and handing his life over to God.

A Sure Thing

Jesus knew that when he bet on God he wasn't gambling. He was placing his "money," and his life, on a sure thing. He literally had nothing to lose, because it's impossible to lose when we let God call the shots. Entrusting to God our lives, our families, our finances, our business, and all we lead isn't like putting our money in the stock market. Even the best companies can head south. But God cannot fail. His will is always the best of all possible options.

I've come to the conclusion that, though Jesus was undeniably fully divine, he did not exercise his power to know all things during his earthly ministry—or at the very least he limited its use. Like us, he had to check in with his Father to get direction. Because he never wanted to drift from his Father's perfect will, he met with him frequently. And because he wanted to carry out that will with courage, he worked through his thoughts and feelings in dialogue with God.

> *God cannot fail. His will is always the best of all possible options.*

Had I been there with Jesus in Gethsemane, I might have been tempted to think that he wasn't able to carry out the job that awaited him. Now I realize it was that very meeting in Gethsemane that empowered him to boldly embrace the cross. His faith was fortified through the time he spent in conversation with his Father.

As you contemplate the leadership challenges you'll face this week, don't put off doing the one thing that will embolden you. Don't procrastinate. Schedule a daily meeting with God during which you speak openly of all that is in your heart and on your mind. After all—you've got nothing to hide and nothing to lose—and everything to gain!

HAVE FAITH!

Have faith! That's the conclusion drawn by a traveler who found a note in a tin can tied to an old pump on a remote desert trail.

Dear Friend,

The pump is all right as of June 1932. I put a new sucker washer into it and it ought to last five years. But the washer dries out and the pump has to be primed. Under the white rock I buried a bottle of water, out of the sun and corked up. There's enough water in it to prime the pump, but not if you drink some first. Pour about one fourth and let her soak to wet the leather. Then pour in the rest medium fast and pump like crazy. You'll get water. The well has never run dry. Have faith. When you get watered up, fill the bottle and put it back as you found it for the next fellar.

Desert Pete

Desert Pete summed up what the wisdom of Jesus teaches us about our relationship with God when he said, "Have faith." That's what it takes to tap into God's power and that's what is cultivated when we make spending time alone with God a top priority. If you want to be a leader who experiences the power of God, there is no shortcut. The strength of your faith will be directly related to the time you spend with God.

But yet another character trait is needed if you're going to be an effective leader. Some have said it's the single trait that will allow average leaders to accomplish great things. It's a trait that characterized Jesus—and it's one we'll take a close look at in the next chapter.

70

THE WISDOM OF JESUS

- Jesus continually trusted in his heavenly Father and tapped into his power.

- Jesus made daily times with his Father a priority.

- Jesus allowed his inner circle to observe him during his moments of greatest vulnerability.

- Jesus poured out his heart to God.

- Jesus was authentic with his heavenly Father.

- Jesus knew he could never lose if he trusted his heavenly Father.

6

FINISH WHAT YOU START

*A*braham Lincoln entered the Blackhawk War as a captain. By the end of the war, he had been *demoted* to the rank of private. Over the course of his life Lincoln suffered two business failures and a nervous breakdown, and he was defeated in nine electoral races before being elected president of the United States. Abraham Lincoln is regarded as one of the greatest leaders in our nation's history—but if he had given up after what seemed like one setback after another, he wouldn't have been remembered at all.

Franklin D. Roosevelt was crippled by polio. Instead of allowing that disability to hold him back, he cultivated a never-give-up attitude that enabled him to become the only United States president elected to four terms.

If he had lacked perseverance Gen. Douglas MacArthur's name wouldn't even warrant a footnote in American history. This great military leader applied for admission to the military academy at West Point and was turned down twice before finally being accepted.

Throughout the course of history this one principle has proven true: Success comes to the committed. Volumes of books could be filled with stories of businesses, inventions, wars, and relationships that were on the verge of failure when a single courageous, persistent person refused to raise the white flag. One more day of business, one more experiment, one more battle, and one more try at communicating a vision proved to be the ticket to success.

No matter whether you're leading your family or a Fortune 500 company, there will be times when you feel like throwing in the towel. Like Lincoln, Roosevelt, and MacArthur, you need endurance. Like a runner on the last leg of a marathon, you need a reservoir of strength to tap . . . a second wind.

Perseverance is of the utmost importance, because without it you'll never see your vision become a reality. Equally important, those you lead need your example of perseverance as a source of encouragement when they're down.

The good news is, while perseverance isn't inherited or handed out in capsule form to be downed with a glass of water, it can be cultivated. Here are three steps that can empower you to become a persevering leader.

STEP ONE:

COUNT THE COST BEFORE MAKING A COMMITMENT

Every week I make a few trips from my home, just south of Portland, Oregon, into the city. And every time I make the trip I ponder four beautiful and spacious condominiums I pass on my way to town. The three-level houses command a spectacular view of the river and are located about ten minutes from the center of the city. What's so impressive about the condominiums isn't their architecture or location; it's the fact that they have stood unfinished for three years. The builder didn't have enough money to finish the project, and now they stand as a mute but powerful testimony to the importance of counting the cost before starting a building.

Jesus wanted his followers to be leaders who finished what they started. That's why he told them up front, "Any of you who does not give up everything he has cannot be my disciple."[1]

By telling the crowds of interested onlookers to count the cost *before* following him, Jesus increased the likelihood they would keep following him when family and friends turned against them, when their good name was slandered, and when their possessions were taken away.

Throughout the course of history this one principle has proven true: Success comes to the committed.

Counting the cost isn't something we only do before choosing to follow Jesus; it's something a leader does before initiating a plan of action. Following Jesus' admonition doesn't necessarily make the process easier; indeed, it takes significant time and effort to calculate the cost before acting. But the price is worth the effort. It enables us to endure hardships because we've factored the price of adversity into our strategy.

The Quitter

I began to learn the lesson of counting the cost through a series of academic setbacks. I was never adept at languages and consequently failed Spanish while in high school. Things didn't get better when I entered college and dropped a Spanish class halfway through the semester because I knew I was going to fail. I would have avoided ever studying a language if the school hadn't required fifteen semester hours of a foreign language in order to graduate.

Now I thought I had it made when a friend told me he had taken Portuguese and found it to be an easy language. "A snap course," he said. Following his advice I signed up for a Portuguese class. It only took me three weeks to discover my friend was wrong. Very wrong. Portuguese wasn't a snap course—it was a killer. Well, once again, instead of taking an F, I did the smart thing. I dropped the class!

The more I thought about my problem the more it made sense for me to study Classical Greek. Because I was planning to attend seminary, where I would have to study both the Greek and Hebrew languages, I decided to learn Greek before going on to graduate school. Over the next year I signed up for two Greek classes, which I dropped after six weeks of study.

The Turning Point

With less than a year to go before graduation, I was running out of time. Determined to pass Greek I signed up again. And yet again I dropped the class. When my wife of four months found out what I had done, she naturally asked me why I had dropped the class. I shuffled my feet and sheepishly said, "I got sick. Remember?"

Cindy put her hands on her hips and with unparalleled grace and sensitivity said, "That isn't true. You did *not* get sick. The problem is you're a quitter!"

Her words stung like a slap across my face. While I didn't like what she had said, her words blew a cloud of self-deception away from my thinking. That was a turning point in my life because I determined right then and there never to give up again. Over the next five years I took two years of Greek and four years of Hebrew—and I managed to maintain an A average. What had changed? Among other things, I learned the value of counting the cost. I entered each challenge with an awareness of the hardships I would encounter, and I resolved not to let them deter me.

Counting the cost isn't something we only do before choosing to follow Jesus; it's something a leader does before initiating a plan of action.

What I learned about perseverance through that experience proved to be one of the most valuable leadership lessons of my life. The application went beyond academics to every major effort I've led, because there always came a time during the process when I wanted out. I suspect as you look back over the teams you've led, you too have shot a longing glance at the exit when the opposition dug in or the resources gave out.

How can you persevere at such times? Before you begin an endeavor, do this: *Count the cost.* Take a piece of paper and make a list of the financial, relational, political, and emotional costs of a decision. Describe a worst-case scenario, and then decide if you're willing to pay that price to finish the process once you've started it. If you are, then go for it—and never look back.

Of course, as you evaluate the cost of moving forward, there's another step you'll need to take.

STEP TWO:

GET GUIDANCE FROM GOD AND LET HIM KEEP YOU ON COURSE

One of the great surprises of my life hasn't been the fact that God directs me down a particular path, but his determination to keep me where I am. When a team of us started South Hills Community Church, we assumed it would explode with growth. When it didn't, we adapted our original strategy, confident that God was about to do something unusual. Of course, "unusual" in our minds meant rapid growth. In an effort to stimulate expansion, we put to use many of the tried and proven methods of church growth. We pounded on the gate of heaven, pleading with God to do something, yet the church did not grow numerically.

Learning to Stay Put

Meanwhile, ministries in other parts of the country would periodically contact me to see if I would consider a move. On every occasion the sinking feeling in the pit of my stomach revealed to me that I should stay put. Refusing to base my decision on feelings alone, I entered the process of interviews and an occasional personal visit or two. While many of these churches offered more resources and influence, I never felt God releasing me from my current post.

At times I would become frustrated and angry with God. I couldn't figure out why he wanted me to remain in a place of service where I was seeing so little visible fruit. But long ago I had determined two things: First, I would never go somewhere unless I truly felt God directing me. Second, I would never give up unless I believed God had released me.

I have found these resolutions to be a crucial element of perseverance. Like everybody else, I don't like emotional pain. As a visionary leader I agonize when the ship I'm sailing can't seem to catch any wind and move forward. And yes, I admit I like it a lot when the captains of other ships see the beauty and speed of *my* craft.

Of course, I realize there are times when God directs leaders to go from one place to another in rapid succession. Such leaders often serve as catalysts for a rapid turnaround. Or they may have particular expertise in the start-up phase of a business or church.

One of the great surprises of my life hasn't been the fact that God directs me down a particular path, but his determination to keep me where I am.

Often such leaders become restless when things reach a certain stage and begin to sense God nudging them on to another challenge.

The Myth of the Greener Grass

Having said that, I believe most leaders at least periodically suffer from the myth of the greener grass. Haven't there been times in your life when you thought things looked better on the other side of the fence? In your drive to succeed, haven't you dreamed of a field with less hardship and more rewards? There may very well have been occasions when you've climbed over a fence without looking up and getting God's approval.

If you've ever longed for a better world, then you'll have no trouble understanding why the man Jesus delivered from a host of demons wanted to follow him.[2] For years the man had been bound with chains and kept under guard. Yet, the power of the demons enabled him to snap the chains and flee to underground tombs.

After Jesus healed the man, he begged to travel with Jesus. No wonder! What better way to show his appreciation than to be a part of Jesus' support team? And what a powerful impact his story would have on others who were investigating the claims of Jesus!

But God had a different plan. Jesus told him to go home. Obviously from that man's perspective he was missing out on the action. He may very well have felt that Jesus had just sent him away with a poor Plan B. Yet Luke tells us that this man who had been given a new lease on life "went away and told all over town how much Jesus had done for him."[3]

Red Light . . . Green Light

It may be that you need to know right now if God is releasing you from your current leadership role so you can pursue another one. If you do, I'd suggest there are four "traffic lights" that must be green before you feel the freedom to leave.

First, determine if your motivation is to escape a problem—or to pursue a fresh vision God has given you. If you're just trying to escape a burning building, be careful. Because failure is the seed of success, it just may be that the lessons you are learning in your current situation will equip you for later success. Running away is seldom the best solution.

Second, determine if you can make the move and still hold to your core values. God never asks us to leave one leadership position so we can assume another one that will cause us to abandon our core values. And even if a core value isn't threatened, be sure no biblical principle is compromised.

Third, seek wise counsel. One reason effective leaders make consistently good decisions is because they gain insight

78

from others. Avoid seeking advice from people who will only tell you what you want to hear.

Fourth, ask God for guidance. As we've seen, Jesus spent significant chunks of time with his Father in prayer. While I've never heard the audible voice of God telling me what to do, I have sensed whether a course of action is consistent with his will. How can I tell? If I've taken the above action and sense no resistance, then I know that the decision is morally acceptable to God and supported by wise counsel. If in spite of having followed these steps I have a sinking feeling in my gut, I know that God is not behind the move. On the other hand, if as I pray I have a growing sense of excitement and peace, then I know that God is nudging me forward.

> *Hope has the power to infuse us with energy in even the most challenging situations.*

I've learned that if all four lights are *not* green God wants me to stay where I am (I'll talk more about decision making in chapter 9). Leaving is no longer an option. The only option is to lead with diligence. The next step will enable you to do so with enthusiasm.

Step Three:

Cultivate Hope That the Vision Will Become Reality

One evening a father was driving home from work when he stopped to watch his son play in a Little League baseball game. As he sat down behind the dugout on the first-base side of the field, he asked his son, "What's the score?"

"We're behind 14 to nothing," his son shouted back.

"Really? Well, you don't look very discouraged."

"Discouraged?" his son asked with a puzzled look. "Why should I be discouraged? We haven't been up to bat yet."

That boy wasn't discouraged because he believed the best was yet to come. Hope has the power to infuse us with energy in even the most challenging situations. Our problem so often is we *know* it's important to possess hope, but we don't know *how* to nurture it. And often when we need hope the most, it seems out of reach—like a forgotten combination to a lock. Let me share two ways we can cultivate the kind of hope that will help us persevere.

FIRST, FOCUS ON THE *BLOW YOUR SOCKS OFF VISION.*

Nothing could have been more discouraging for Jesus' disciples than his impending death. In the face of his departure, Jesus made a promise he knew would equip them to hang in there when they felt like bailing out. He told them that his death was not a final farewell. Like a trailblazer, he was going ahead of them to the Father's house so he could prepare a place for them.[4] He wanted them to know that they could look forward with unwavering confidence to a better tomorrow.

Several years ago I read about an experiment in which researchers placed a dozen laboratory mice in a vat of water. As the mice swam in small circles the researchers would periodically lift out of the water several mice who had been identified with a mark on their head. These mice would then be placed back in the water. As the researchers expected, those mice who were lifted out of the water swam far longer than those who hadn't. Why? The researchers concluded that the mice hoped if they could swim just a little longer, they would be delivered in the end. (I've often wondered what really did happen to those mice!)

While we're not mice swimming around in a vat of water, hope is a powerful force that can enable us to keep swimming when our muscles ache and our arms are tired. Jesus' word of hope must have been so encouraging to the disciples, as it is for us: "I will come back and take you to be with me that you also may be where I am."[5]

Don't fixate on the obstacles you face. Instead, focus on the *Blow Your Socks Off Vision* you hope to become a reality.

SECOND, IDENTIFY HOW THE HARDSHIP WILL MAKE YOU STRONGER.

Jesus also promised that we would make it through adversity and come out stronger on the other side. It's a lesson Peter learned the hard way. During the final hours before the betrayal and arrest, Jesus told Peter, "Satan has asked to sift you as wheat. But I have prayed for you, Simon, that your faith may not fail. And when you have turned back, strengthen your brothers."[6]

Very Bad News

The words of Jesus to Peter remind me of the story of a doctor who called a patient and said, "John, I've got bad news and really bad news."

"Oh no!" John said. "Give me the bad news first."

"The bad news is that I've gotten back the results of your tests and you have forty-eight hours to live."

"Wait a minute," John shouted into the phone. "If that's the bad news, what could be worse?"

"I forgot to call you yesterday," the doctor murmured quietly.

I suspect when Peter heard the Lord's announcement about his future testing, he felt like somebody had just kicked the slats out from under his bed. I can imagine the fisherman looking up, tilting his head quizzically, and asking, "Lord, are you telling me you've given Satan permission to sift me as wheat?"

"Right!" came the immediate reply.

"And the part about 'when I turn back,' that means I'm going to turn away from you?"

"Right again."

That's bad news and very bad news. Peter would be sifted as wheat *and* he would fall away. But embedded in the message were words of hope. Jesus also said, "*When* you have turned back." Peter would survive the ordeal. And he would later be used to strengthen the brothers. Not only would he survive the ordeal, but he would actually be stronger as a result.

81

The Purpose of Trials

James, the half brother of Jesus, made it clear that the purpose of all testing is to build perseverance.[7] Instead of looking at the disappointments we face, we look beyond the hardship to the strength of character it will produce in our lives.

But the outcome is by no means certain. There is no guarantee that adversity will develop character. That only happens *if* we choose to trust God. That's why Jesus told Peter, "I have prayed for you, Simon, that your faith may not fail."[8] Jesus knew that hardship could surely strengthen Peter's character—provided he would maintain his faith in God. Such a spiritual reality changes how we view adversity.

That's why James told his readers, "Consider it pure joy, my brothers, whenever you face trials."[9]

Can you read those words without slamming on your mental brakes? I can't. The first time I read that line I misunderstood its meaning. I thought he was saying something like, "Rejoice that you have cancer. Be happy your dog just died. Have a party to celebrate your business failure."

On the surface that does appear to be what he's saying. But a deeper look reveals something significant. James did not urge us to be joyful *because of* the trials we face. Instead, he urged us to find joy *in the outcome* of those trials. We don't celebrate problems; we celebrate the fact that God can use problems to make us better people, to make us better leaders. Adversity does for our soul what weight lifting does for our body. It makes us stronger. It empowers us to finish what we start.

If you're like me you'd prefer developing internal strength without pain. But that's just not possible. There are no detours around suffering. Every leader will encounter hardship and disappointment. You'll experience the betrayal of a friend. You'll face seemingly endless delays. You'll know the pain of having well-thought-out strategies fall flat. While you can't avoid hardship, you *can* choose to cultivate joy in the midst of setbacks—by believing that God will use them to strengthen your character. That's the great hope you must rivet your attention on, like a guiding star, to help you make it through dark nights.

Winners Never Quit!

If you're a leader there will most assuredly be times you will feel the challenges are too great ... the obstacles too high

... the problems too tough ... the conflicts too painful. Always remember that men and women who persevered attained the greatest accomplishments in world history. They were leaders who allowed hardship to strengthen their resolve, leaders who believed that if they would keep on trying, they would emerge victorious.

Adversity does for our soul what weight lifting does for our body. It makes us stronger. It empowers us to finish what we start.

The Wright brothers, Orville and Wilbur, wanted to do more than repair bicycles—so they dreamed of a machine they could ride across the sky. Determined to follow their dream, they made history when the first power-driven airplane puttered into the sky on December 17, 1903.

Daniel Webster was not by nature a gifted communicator. But after years of hard work he became one of America's greatest orators.

George Washington lost more battles than he won during the American Revolution, but he led the nation to victory and became the first president of the United States.

John Bunyan wrote *Pilgrim's Progress* while languishing in the Bedford prison in England where he was suffering because of his religious views.

Robert Burns was an illiterate Scottish country boy who became a famous poet. Short-story writer O. Henry was a criminal and an outcast. The great German composer Ludwig van Beethoven was deaf. The English poet John Milton was blind.

And then there was Elmo McGringle. I bet you've never heard of him, have you? That's because he quit.

∞

THE WISDOM OF JESUS

- Jesus demanded that potential disciples count the cost before following him.

- Jesus focused the attention of his disciples on his *Blow Your Socks Off Vision.*

- Jesus knew that hardship would only make his followers stronger.

7

BRIDLE YOUR APPETITES

Whatever your struggle may be—an appetite for pleasure, money, power, or fame—it's crucial you learn to bridle it. A single uncontrolled character flaw can undermine your greatest accomplishments. And nobody is immune from the danger.

I remember talking with a church leader who told me he didn't think he could ever commit a sexual sin. "I mean a big one," he explained. "You know . . . like having an affair or sleeping with a hooker."

I paused for a moment and then asked, "So . . . you think you're stronger than Samson, godlier than David, and wiser than Solomon?"

He stood silently for so long I thought he hadn't heard my question. And then he pushed his glasses up the bridge of his nose and said, "I never thought of it like that before."

Consider the struggles of these great leaders:

- With Noah it was alcohol.
- With Lot it was greed.
- With Jacob it was deception.

- With Moses it was anger.

- With Samson, David, and Solomon it was lust.

- With Peter it was fear.

These men weren't second-string leaders. They were lead-off hitters. They were impact players. Yet each one failed to shore up their weakness, and it cost them dearly.

My goal in this chapter is to set out a strategy that can help you develop the self-discipline needed to protect you from yourself, a plan that can keep you from spoiling what you're trying to accomplish. After years of research and the publication of two books on compulsive behavior, I've identified three essential elements, with important insights drawn from the wisdom of Jesus. By no means do I intend to imply that these principles are all you need to know, but I'm confident that if you put them into practice, they will help you bridle your most destructive appetites.

A single uncontrolled character flaw can undermine your greatest accomplishments.

THE FIRST ELEMENT:

PERSPECTIVE

One day a young man was driving his red Mazda Miata on a winding country road along the Pacific coast in northern California. As the afternoon sun warmed his face and the wind ruffled his hair he came around a turn only to find a dilapidated pickup heading straight for him. The young man quickly jerked the steering wheel to the right and swerved around the pickup. As he passed, a woman shouted at him through the open window, "Pig!"

Without delay he yelled at her, "Jerk!"

A moment later he barely missed the three-hundred-pound pig standing in the middle of the road. In that moment he experienced a fresh perspective . . . a new way of seeing things!

When it comes to your area of greatest weakness, the weak chink in your armor, you need a similar experience . . . a fresh perspective. It may be you're not heeding certain warnings because you don't comprehend the danger you face. You may be entering a moral battle that you think you can win alone. Or you may have been struggling for some time and are convinced you will never be able to win the battle. In either case, you may find it valuable to gain new insights about yourself and your struggle.

The Nature of Temptation

It's crucial to understand that there is nothing innately wrong with temptation. It's something each of us encounters on a daily basis. Jesus himself faced temptation during his life here on earth. When Jesus taught us to ask God not to lead us into temptation,[1] he was not suggesting that God would ever lead us into sin. Nor did he mean that temptation can be avoided altogether. Instead, I interpret his words to mean that we should ask God to prevent us from having the inclination and opportunity to sin at the same time.

In order for that prayer to be answered, we must cooperate with God and do at least these two things: first, control our inclinations, and second, do all we can to control our environment.

Control Your Inclinations

Jesus didn't pull any punches when he said, "No one can serve two masters. Either he will hate the one and love the other, or he will be devoted to the one and despise the other."[2] While Jesus was talking about the tension between loving God and loving money, the principle applies to other areas of life as well. We cannot devote ourselves to God and at the same time nurture a secret sin. Nor can we devote ourselves to a *Blow Your Socks Off Vision* that requires leading with integrity while living a double life.

You may be thinking, "Wait a minute, Bill, so what if I pick up a *Playboy* once in a while; I've never committed adultery."

Or "Just because I pad my expense account, that doesn't make me a thief." You may rationalize your behavior—whether it has something to do with sex, drugs, money, or power—by denying its seriousness.

You must control your destructive inclinations by staying away from "little sins," because in reality they aren't so little—and they can and often do lead to destruction.

The truth is, you must control your destructive inclinations by staying away from "little sins," because in reality they *aren't* so little—and they *can* and often do lead to destruction. The apostle Paul said, "Don't you know that when you offer yourselves to someone to obey him as slaves, you are slaves to the one whom you obey—whether you are slaves to sin, which leads to death, or to obedience, which leads to righteousness."[3]

DON'T PET THE GREMLIN

In effect, Paul is telling us that our pet pleasure—whatever it may be—is a gremlin. Do you remember those cute furry creatures from the movie? They start out soft and cuddly, and before long they turn into monsters that destroy life.

A man or woman who is lonely, bored, stressed out, or depressed may turn to a substance, like alcohol or drugs, or to a behavior, like gambling or sex, to create a mood swing. Initially these things may seem harmless. But the law of diminishing returns tells us it takes more and more of the substance and a riskier behavior to create the mood swing. This painful reality demands we control our evil inclinations by determining not to allow them a foothold in our lives. We must make up our minds to serve God and not our passion for pleasure, power, fame, or fortune.

It may be that such a resolution hasn't been easy for you to make—or it's more likely you've discovered that it's almost impossible to keep. So let's peel back the surface and take the issue to the next level. Jesus made it clear that demonic powers entice us to do evil. You may recall that when Peter battled with the fear of being unveiled as a follower of Jesus, it was Satan who used that circumstance to tempt him to deny he knew Jesus.[4]

DON'T SERVE AN IDOL

Ultimately Satan wants us to turn our back on the one true God and worship him. That's what he sought from Jesus in the temptation in the desert,[5] and it's what he seeks from us yet today. Of course, he's smart enough to know most of us won't worship him directly—but he doesn't care how he gets it. If he can convince us to substitute a counterfeit god for the real thing, he has us right where he wants us.

An idol is anything we trust besides God to meet our deepest needs.

By now you may be thinking, "Bill, are you one of those guys who sees a demon behind every bush? Do you blame the devil for all your struggles?"

The answer to both questions is an emphatic no! But I do take the devil seriously. I think he's real, and I believe he's tricked us into *not* taking him seriously—treating him, it would seem, like a declawed tiger.

I'm convinced many of us in the Western world have so divorced the supernatural from our lives that we live as though this realm is not real. Many of us pay lip service to the presence of the devil and his demonic army, but in practice these spiritual forces of evil seem no more threatening than a hole in the ozone layer.

I want to challenge you to realize that you as a leader have an enemy who is out to destroy you. And he does that by redirecting your love to an illusion that offers you pleasure, power, fame, or fortune. He'll use such things as:

- a flirtatious relationship with a coworker.
- a casual look at an erotic magazine or web site.
- an occasional padding of an expense account.

Don't let yourself minimize what's happening in your life. An obsession with anything other than God is idolatry.

I realize I'm playing hardball with you. You may be thinking, "Bill, now you've gone too far. It's one thing to have a little pet sin. But an idol? How could you suggest such a thing?"

I can suggest it because my thinking is based on the truth of God's Word. We tend to view an idol as an image in the shape of a man, woman, or animal. But an idol is anything we trust besides God to meet our deepest needs. It can be any substance we use or behavior we act out in order to create a mood swing when we're bored or depressed. It can be power, fame, or fortune when we look to them for our significance or security.

While such practices seem destructive enough in themselves, the apostle Paul ripped off their mask and exposed an ugly monster when he said there is a demon behind every idol.[6] Ultimately, when we let our base appetites go unchecked, we're handing the reins of our life over to an evil spirit. Worse than that, we're worshiping a false god and becoming intertwined with the demon that energizes it.

RECOGNIZE THE SPIRITUAL HIERARCHY

As a leader it's important to recognize there is a spiritual hierarchy that's as defined as anything in the physical world. Jesus praised the faith of a Roman centurion who had asked him to heal his servant. When the Lord agreed to go to the man's home, the soldier declined a personal visit. He urged Jesus to "just say the word, and my servant will be healed."[7]

The centurion based his conclusion on the fact that he was a man under the authority of a superior, the emperor. When the centurion spoke, he spoke with the emperor's authority, and so those under his command obeyed his every order. Similarly, Jesus, as one vested with God's authority, didn't need to go to the man's house, because he could simply give the command and the centurion's servant would be healed. Why? Because the illness, or the evil spirit causing the illness, would obey Jesus' command to leave the boy. Similarly, Jesus has authority over evil forces that attack us. Yet his power is neutralized if we choose to place ourselves under the dominion of the powers of this dark world.

Once you grasp this awe-inspiring truth, you'll understand why it's so hard to break free from a compulsion. And you'll realize why things can so quickly go from bad to worse. I hope you'll also grasp why you must control your evil inclinations. The alternative is a life devoted to something that violates your core values and prevents you from realizing your driving purpose and pursuing your *Blow Your Socks Off Vision.*

LET'S TALK

I wish I could pull up a comfortable chair and sit beside you. For just a moment I would ask you to be honest with yourself and with God. If your life is under control, I would urge you to keep it that way. But if it isn't, I would beg you to deal with your problem before it destroys you.

If we were talking face-to-face, you would sense the absolute seriousness of my tone, a tone created by the memory of two men. The first served as pastor of a large and influential church; the other served as pastor of a fast-growing church in California.

Each invited me to speak to his congregation, and each listened attentively as I shared what you've just read. They repeatedly nodded their heads in agreement. I could see their support when I urged each person in the audience to break free from any idol or evil spirit that had captured their soul. What I couldn't see was the secret sin they were hiding. Each had lost control of his life. One had successfully covered his sins for two decades; the other had done so for six months. Today both are sitting on the sidelines after leaving the field in dishonor, their ministries devastated and their reputations destroyed.

Please, for the sake of God's reputation, for the sake of your own, for the sake of your family, friends, and those you lead— break free today. Don't allow all you've invested your life in to be tarnished because you were too proud, too independent, or too fearful to act decisively. As a leader, resolve to keep your appetites under control. If that means acknowledging that they aren't, then admit it. Make the tough call, and then tell a trusted friend. Seek help—and seek it now.

Taking that step is crucial, and it will lead you to the next one.

Control Your Environment

I'm convinced we often invite temptation inside when it knocks on our door because we haven't devised a strategy for sending it away. We frequently swear off a bad habit. We promise God we'll never embrace temptation again, but we fail to remove the doorbell and welcome mat. We may not even close the door. And then when temptation strolls in the door and whispers in our ear, we all too often and all too eagerly listen.

AVOID TRIGGERS

One thing that works to our advantage is the fact that sin follows a consistent pattern. There are no exceptions. Jesus summarized the process when he said, "The good man brings good things out of the good stored up in him, and the evil man brings evil things out of the evil stored up in him."[8]

We often invite temptation inside when it knocks on our door because we haven't devised a strategy for sending it away.

The process is pretty straightforward, isn't it? Sinful actions begin with sinful thoughts. One thing I so admire about Jesus' teaching is that he breaks complex problems down to their simplest elements. What could be simpler: Bad behavior follows bad thinking like stink follows a skunk. We fanaticize about something sensually appealing or something self-serving—and then we act.

James, the half brother of Jesus, must have learned a lot as he grew up with Jesus. Perhaps that's why he amplified Jesus' teaching with the words, "Each one is tempted when, by his own evil desire, he is dragged away and enticed. Then, after desire has conceived, it gives birth to sin; and sin, when it is full-grown, gives birth to death."[9] Notice the progression:

ENTICEMENT (Thoughts) → CONCEPTION (Triggers) → SIN → DEATH

We begin by thinking of a substance or behavior that will create a mood swing—something that will make us feel better fast. It may be something as seemingly harmless as a delicious dessert or as obviously harmful as heroin. It could be a one-night stand or a misuse of company funds. The more we think about it the more we want to act on our impulses. But instead of leaping from the thought to the act in one big step, we may take a small step ... or a series of small steps. These small steps are triggers.

For someone with an eating compulsion the trigger may be buying the ingredients for brownies to make a treat for the kids. For the sex addict it could be surfing the Internet or calling a former girlfriend or boyfriend "just to talk." For the alcoholic it may be visiting a local pub for a soft drink.

Each of us has unique rituals or triggers that must be avoided. Once the trigger is pulled we can no more stop the process than we can catch a discharged bullet, send it back down the barrel of a gun, and return it to its shell casing.

After the Monica Lewinsky situation broke, I participated in a series of marathon radio and television interviews. One of the most frequently asked questions was this: "How can the president find freedom from his sexual addiction?"

The answer was relatively simple, but surely not easy. I responded, "He has to do the same thing everyone else does. He has to identify his triggers and get rid of them."

TAKE DECISIVE STEPS

While counseling and prayer are undeniably important, a person must also take decisive steps to eliminate or avoid those situations that trigger sinful behavior. Use the following chart,

93

or one like it, to help you devise a strategy to do away with
those triggers.

Triggers	How I'll Avoid Them
1._____	1._____
2._____	2._____
3._____	3._____
4._____	4._____
5._____	5._____
6._____	6._____

Your ability to bridle your appetites will be directly related
to your willingness to act decisively and assertively. Remember the words of Jesus: "No one can serve two masters."[10] As
this spiritual perspective begins to govern your conduct, you
may wonder what you'll substitute for the behavior you have
been turning to for so long. In any event I hope that's what
you're wondering—because that question leads to the second
element of the strategy for success.

The Second Element:

Presence

If you're a leader, then you're most likely intimately
acquainted with loneliness. I don't mean you're lacking in
friends. Indeed, friends and associates may surround you;
crowds may follow you. But nobody else knows the pressures
you face, the responsibilities you bear, and the heartaches you
suffer. There are decisions only you can make and consequences you alone must bear.

Because leaders typically perceive that others can't identify
with their unique pressures, they tend to live in emotional iso-

lation. Being vulnerable and opening up to others is like pushing an eight-feet-tall, two-hundred-pound medicine ball up a hill. Progress is slow and painful. And it's got a dangerous downside. If you're transparent you might give an edge to the competition—or others might interpret your honesty about your struggles as a sign of weakness.

Because leaders typically perceive that others can't identify with their unique pressures, they tend to live in emotional isolation.

Those two hazards help explain why so many pastors and politicians refuse to share their personal struggles with others—even close friends. I've had scores of pastors tell me they don't have a single person in their church with whom they can talk openly. The next time you're in a bookstore, take note of the exposés written by aides, which reveal the secrets of government officials for whom they once worked. No wonder politicians keep even their closest associates at arm's length!

Recognize the Counterfeit

Such isolation can cause a leader to feel justified in turning for comfort to whatever nurtured him or her in the past. Whether it's illicit sex, food, money, drugs, compulsive work, or alcohol—these things only provide an illusion of intimacy . . . a counterfeit. But when we choose the illusion over real intimacy, we cut ourselves off from God and from those we need the most. The image is so absurd it's beyond

When we choose the illusion over real intimacy, we cut ourselves off from God and from those we need the most.

95

ridiculous. It's like a mother who cherishes a baby's photograph and starves her child, or a man who dances with a mannequin and ignores his wife.

When we come to our senses and toss out the counterfeits, we need to replace them with the real thing. Jesus alone can meet our deepest needs, because he alone understands our struggles. Think about it: As a leader he faced important decisions, relational conflicts, misunderstanding, desertion, betrayal, and crucifixion. In the midst of all this he had the responsibility of validating his message and identity while nurturing his disciples so they could take his message to the world.

Yet, even when facing all that pressure, he never once turned to an illusion for comfort. Jesus always allowed his heavenly Father to meet his needs. With the shadow of the cross looming over him, he told his Father, "I pray also for those who will believe in me through their [his disciples'] message, that all of them may be one, Father, just as you are in me and I am in you. May they also be in us."[11]

Jesus offered us what he had—a relationship with the One who understands our struggles and is always there when we need him. As a leader you are never alone. Never! This truth is so important that Jesus reiterated it often to his disciples. In the upper room he said, "I will not leave you as orphans; I will come to you."[12] After his resurrection Jesus said, "I am with you always, to the very end of the age."[13]

How close is Jesus when you need him? He's closer than your shadow or the sunlight on your face. He's as close as your breath. A recognition of his presence changes everything. It gives us access to the One who can meet our deepest needs. And it leads us to the final element of the strategy that can give you what you need in order to bridle your appetites.

THE THIRD ELEMENT:

POWER

96 | The biggest and most joyous surprise I experienced after trusting Jesus to forgive me and give me eternal life was receiving his power to change me. Habits that had controlled me like a boa constrictor wrapped around a rabbit were suddenly shed. I didn't choose to follow Jesus until I was in college, so some of those habits were deeply ingrained. Yet through his power they fell away.

Initially, I thought the Christian life would be as smooth as skates across ice. And then reality hit. The deadly grip of those habits may have been broken, but the force that drove them still lurked in a cave in the corner of my mind. All they needed to take over my life again was the right trigger. It was then I discovered that the power of Jesus was a force I had to tap into, or else it was as useless as batteries in a box.

Yes, Jesus was present. But how could I utilize his presence to give me victory? The words Jesus spoke to his disciples give us the best answer there is. He told them, "I am the vine; you are the branches. If a man remains in me and I in him, he will bear much fruit; apart from me you can do nothing."[14]

The imagery Jesus uses is once again profound in its simplicity. I am to relate to him as a branch relates to a vine. I am to draw life and strength from him. As I do so, he produces fruit that I bear to the Father's glory.

When I tap into my evil nature, it produces all sorts of evil fruit. The rotten fruit is symptomatic of the reality that I'm no longer drawing on the life and power of Jesus. What am I to do? I'm to thank God that he has saved me from a life of bondage to sin and trust Jesus to once more live his life through me.

Focus Your Faith on Jesus

You might be surprised how well the strategy of drawing on the power of Jesus works. When I vow to never act compulsively again, I'm focusing on myself, on what I *won't* do, instead of on Jesus. Such thinking only leads to further obsessive thinking and compulsive behavior. It's like trying to stop thinking of a white elephant with red spots by telling yourself, "I will not think of white elephants with red spots. I will not think of white elephants with red spots." By making such a vow I'm actually doing the very thing I'm trying to stop doing.

Instead, we need to acknowledge our destructive patterns and focus our attention on the power available to us through Jesus.

The Willamette Valley in Oregon is home to some of the finest wine country in North America. I was recently touring one of the vineyards when I passed by a plant that was sobbing softly. I stopped dead in my tracks and listened.

"Why can't I bear sumptuous grapes?" it cried.

As I looked at the grief-stricken branch I saw a dewdrop fall from a scrawny grape.

As I contemplated how to comfort the branch the gardener interrupted my thoughts. He stepped past me and grabbed the branch with his left hand and cut it off with the clippers he held in his right hand. He then took the branch and grafted it into another vine a row over.

Jesus is not only present when we need him, he's willing to infuse us with his strength and to fortify our character.

The gardener then looked at me, winked, and said, "He'll bear good fruit now. He's attached to one of the healthiest plants in the vineyard."

What that imaginary gardener (all right, I admit I made up this story!) did for that branch, God does for those who choose to follow Jesus.

Jesus told his disciples that the awe-inspiring power of God is available to us right now through faith. Jesus is not only present when we need him, he's willing to infuse us with his strength and to fortify our character.

A FRESH PERSPECTIVE

I began this chapter with the promise to share three elements aimed at helping you bridle your destructive appetites. As we apply what we're learning, we'll take the fresh insights about the benefits and consequences of our choices and develop a strategy to help us tap into God's power.

I'm reminded of the story about the company president who wanted to enroll his employees in a new group insurance plan. The only condition the insurance company placed on his business was that every employee enroll in the program. After educating his employees about the benefits of the program and answering their questions, he asked them all to sign up.

When the registration forms were counted, the president discovered one employee had not filled out his form. After identifying the man, he had his assistant meet with him. A short time later the assistant returned without the form.

"He's not interested," he reported.

Over the next several weeks the president had several other employees meet with the holdout; he even had a salesman from the insurance company meet with him. But nobody had any success in changing his mind.

Finally the president called the man into his office and asked him very politely to please hand in his registration form.

"But, sir," the man said. "I don't want to participate in the new program. I like the old one better."

"You may do whatever you want," the president said softly. "But if you don't sign up, you'll be fired."

The man immediately sat down, filled out the application, handed it to the boss, and left. Moments later he saw a friend and told him he had finally decided to go along with the new insurance plan. When his friend asked what had changed his mind, he said, "Nobody ever explained it to me quite like that."

That reluctant participant had a fresh perspective that altered his thinking and his motivation. I sincerely hope you receive the same results from reading this chapter.

You're Ready to Build on the Foundation

Perspective, presence, and power are what you need to bridle your appetites and release your potential. Those three elements possess the capacity to strengthen your character and prevent you from doing something reckless that could derail the realization of your *Blow Your Socks Off Vision.*

While character is the foundation of leadership, competency is the building itself. Having laid the foundation, we're ready to move on to the next section, where you'll discover how to unleash the skills needed to become an effective leader.

THE WISDOM OF JESUS

- Jesus urged his followers to ask God to never allow them to have the *inclination* and *opportunity* to sin at the same time.

- Jesus knew a person couldn't be devoted to God and nurture a secret sin at the same time.

- Jesus recognized the evil spirits behind evil actions.

- Jesus knew that pure thoughts are the source of pure actions.

- Jesus always allowed his heavenly Father to meet his needs.

- Jesus promised to give us strength when we're tempted.

PART TWO

Awaken Your Skills

A tree is recognized by its fruit.

Jesus of Nazareth—Matthew 12:33

8

KEEP THE VISION ALIVE

*A*s a leader you'll never achieve success because you've been pulled there. Instead, those you lead will lift you to success, like wind beneath an eagle's wings.

Successfully bringing your vision into reality requires the enthusiastic support and cooperation of those alongside and underneath you. As a leader you must inspire them to do things they would not do unless they were being led.

While every leader knows that it's important to inspire his or her team, only one in ten leaders believe they are truly inspirational. In fact, when asked what leadership skill they find most difficult to master, men and women overwhelmingly identified the ability to inspire a shared vision as the hardest practice to learn.[1]

That's the bad news. The good news is inspirational leaders consistently do, as Jesus did, the same kinds of things to inspire people. In this chapter you'll discover the three most important characteristics of an inspirational leader. These principles aren't complicated—and they do work. If you put them into practice you will almost without fail see an improvement in morale that will lift you, and those you lead, to higher levels of success.

PRINCIPLE ONE:

INSPIRATIONAL LEADERS ARE FOCUSED

Robert Ballard wanted to see something that had rested on the bottom of the Atlantic Ocean for almost seventy-five years. Even though he was a respected scientist with an unparalleled track record, he couldn't find investors to provide the $1.5 million needed to carry out an expedition to locate the *R.M.S. Titanic.* Eventually, after successfully locating two nuclear submarines that had sunk in the 1960s, Ballard received word that the United States Navy was willing to let him use their equipment to search for *Titanic.*

Those you lead will lift you to success, like wind beneath an eagle's wings.

Finding the 882-foot ship proved more difficult than he had ever imagined. His team first tried to locate it with a sonar torpedo dragged back and forth across the ocean floor. Later they searched the ocean floor with a video camera.

Instead of giving up, Ballard changed his tactics. Rather than look for the hull of the ship, he began to search for the comet-tail debris trail that he estimated would be almost a mile long. His diligence paid off. On September 1, 1985, his nighttime crew spotted one of *Titanic*'s giant boilers.

One would think with such a dramatic discovery investors would have lined up with money to throw at the project. They didn't. It took Ballard another year to raise the necessary funds in order to visit *Titanic*'s grave. Thirteen long years after the search began, Robert Ballard finally beheld the ship he had devoted so much time and energy to finding.

Make a Difference

As I read about Ballard's historic discovery, the question that welled up in my mind was this: "What enabled Robert Ballard to keep the interest and loyalty of his team?" The answer may surprise you. Robert Ballard didn't inspire his team with the promise of finding a sunken ship. He inspired them with a dream of doing something important to the world, something that would give us a window into the past, something that would finally answer some nagging questions. He led his team through danger and discouragement with the hope that they could do something that would give meaning to their lives.[2]

Without exception, inspirational leaders possess a compelling vision of the future that is greater than any single event or experience. Billy Graham didn't inspire his team with the thought of massive crusades. He inspired them with a vision of sharing the gospel with as many people as possible in as many countries as possible.

Martin Luther King Jr. had a vision of an America where blacks and whites lived together without racial barriers. His vision inspired men, women, and children across America to risk their lives as they stood up for racial equality.

> *Inspirational leaders possess a compelling vision of the future that is greater than any single event or experience.*

James Dobson dreamed of a country where the family is viewed as a sacred unit. His radio program, aired daily on 1,600 stations, has inspired loyal listeners across America to work tirelessly to advance the rights of families.

The Hewlett-Packard company didn't set out to make printers but "to make technical contributions for the advancement and welfare of humanity." That driving purpose has inspired some of the most brilliant high-tech minds in the world to produce a vast assortment of products.

Once you've identified your *Blow Your Socks Off Vision*, you must continually communicate it to everyone on your team. Inspirational leaders can be introverts or extroverts; they can be male or female, tall or short, physically attractive or just plain average. But they will, without exception, be people who cause those around them to *continually* think about the vision they hope to bring into reality.

Adapt the Message

Time and again Jesus reminded his disciples that his mission, his driving purpose, was to seek and to save lost people. On the day he called his first disciples he said, "I will make you fishers of men."[3] When he recruited Levi (also known as Matthew), he said, "I have not come to call the righteous, but sinners to repentance."[4]

Jesus was so consumed with his vision, so committed to it, that he repeatedly took advantage of real-life situations to communicate it. After speaking with the Samaritan woman at the well, Jesus told his disciples, "Open your eyes and look at the fields! They are ripe for harvest."[5] After Zacchaeus humbled himself, Jesus stated his mission in the clearest of terms: "The Son of Man came to seek and to save what was lost."[6]

> *As leaders we must lock on to our vision and adapt our message to each situation.*

Jesus frequently used teaching situations to instruct his followers about their driving purpose. He spoke of sowing the seed of the word of God into men's hearts,[7] and the great call of disciples everywhere to let their lights shine before others.[8]

Jesus used vivid imagery—and so must we. As leaders we must do more than send out fancy memos about our driving purpose. We must lock on to our vision and adapt our message to each situation.

My friend Bob Farrell has opened over 150 restaurants without a single failure—an amazing accomplishment, given that over eighty percent of all restaurants fail within five years of their opening. His vision was to build restaurants where every employee would be committed to excellent customer service. To communicate his vision Bob asked that every new employee attend a training session. During their time together Bob insisted everyone on the team view the customer not as an intruder but as the boss. He reasoned that since money spent by the customer enabled everyone to keep his or her job, the entire team worked for the customer. Throughout the training session Bob would ask the eager food servers, dishwashers, and managers, "Who's the customer?" and the employees would yell back, "The boss!"

But Bob did more than give pep talks at employee rallies. He communicated the vision personally with every employee. One night a dishwasher didn't show up, so Bob donned an apron and helped the teenager who was washing dishes. He was careful to point out to the high school student that every dish had to be sparkling clean because it was going to be placed in front of the customer. "A sliver of lettuce left on an otherwise clean plate will distract the customer from everything else we have to offer him," Bob said. At Bob's restaurants, dishwashers weren't merely cleaning dirty dishes; they were preparing a sparkling plate for an eager customer waiting to be satisfied.

If you want to inspire those you lead, communicate your vision in terms that relate to them and capture their imagination. Explain how everything they do is important because it helps bring the vision into reality. It includes every aspect, no matter how seemingly mundane—washing dishes, greeting customers, unloading trucks, and answering the phone. Every activity takes on value when it's connected to the vision.

Principle Two:

Inspirational Leaders Are Optimistic

Of course, every leader bumps into walls. I know I have on more occasions than I care to admit. Yet, in spite of bloody noses and stubbed toes, inspirational leaders consistently maintain an optimistic attitude. It's important to understand that neither *optimism* nor *pessimism* defines reality. They are, in fact, *perceptions* of reality.

Optimists, as we are fond of saying, will describe a cup as half full and pessimists will see it as half empty. An optimist looks at the bright side of a situation. They believe that good will come out of even the worst of circumstances. Pessimists anticipate the worst possible outcome. I once had a pessimist tell me, "If you saw things as they *really* are, you'd be a pessimist too!"

Because an attitude of optimism seems crucial to a leader's inspirational ability, I wanted to know more precisely how leaders express optimism. I was pleased to discover that researchers have identified at least three ways in which optimistic leaders inspire their followers.

An Optimistic View of Failure

When something goes wrong, pessimists tend to draw a *general* conclusion based on a single, particular failure. They'll say something like, "This proves that the entire company is messed up!" Or "This just shows that our marriage is no good."

Optimistic leaders respond to failure very differently. Instead of looking for someone to blame, they make it their goal to identify something in the process that caused the failure, so the problem can be corrected and the process improved. Jim Casey, the founder of United Parcel Service, once said, "It's always easier to see difficulties than to develop methods of solving them. But first let us take sight of a goal. The difficulties will be solved in ways we cannot now see."[9]

The impact of this kind of approach can be profound. Instead of leading to name-calling and finger-pointing, it leads to creative and forward-looking interaction. Shortly after I discovered this truth, somebody in my family (I was sure it was my wife) misplaced my car keys. I looked everywhere without success. When Cindy got home, she found me in a pessimistic mood (that's a nice way of saying I was ANGRY). I hurled accusations her way as I impatiently opened one drawer after another in search of the missing keys.

Suddenly I remembered how optimists view failure. I stopped where I stood, looked at Cindy, and said, "I'm sorry. This isn't your fault or mine. The problem is that we don't have a key box."

"A key box?" she asked.

"You know. A place where everybody in the family puts the car keys as soon as they walk in the door."

Immediately the issue changed from "Who lost my keys?" to looking for something we could use as a key box to prevent this "failure" from happening again. Since we implemented the use of a key box, we hardly ever lose keys anymore.

Breakdowns Are Opportunities for Improvement

The ability to view failure optimistically contains the power to transform a communication breakdown into a bridge. Nothing inspires people more than a leader who regards mistakes and failures as opportunities for improvement and growth.

Jesus consistently led by demonstrating an optimistic view of failure. Consider the scene described by John in which the religious leaders of Jesus' day took a woman caught in adultery and brought her to the temple courts where Jesus was teaching a crowd of people.[10] They demanded that Jesus render a judgment on this woman.

> *The ability to view failure optimistically contains the power to transform a communication breakdown into a bridge.*

Instead of pointing a finger of condemnation, Jesus gave permission for any one of them who was without sin to throw the first stone. The religious leaders silently slunk away.

When they had all left, Jesus turned to the woman and said, "Woman, where are they? Has no one condemned you?" "No one, sir," she answered. Jesus responded with these words:

"Then neither do I condemn you. . . . Go now and leave your life of sin."[11]

Jesus took this woman's awful failure and turned it into an opportunity for forgiveness and growth. Every disciple who saw their leader confront that situation had to have been inspired to extend forgiveness to others and turn failures into opportunities for growth.

An Optimistic View of Success

SHARE CENTER STAGE

Because pessimists don't expect to succeed, they're usually amazed when victory occurs. Consequently, they like to occupy center stage at the awards ceremony. Instead of sharing the spotlight with teammates, they prefer basking in it alone. After all, they must figure, they'll very likely never be on a winning team again so they might as well enjoy the moment.

Not so with optimistic leaders. They believe that if they lead diligently and wisely, they will succeed. It may take a while, but eventually they'll capture success, like a sail catching the wind. Once they do find success, or success finds them, they evaluate how it happened and then go on to predict more victories in the future.

I remember the moment after the Chicago Bulls won their fifth National Basketball Association title. A reporter shoved a microphone in Michael Jordan's face and asked, "How did you do it? How did you win five titles?"

"What did you expect?" Jordan snarled. "I'm the greatest man to ever put on a pair of Nikes. Hey, they even named a shoe after me. You know—the *Air Jordan*. Remember, I'm Mike. The kids all say, 'I wanna be like Mike.' We won because of me! Me! Me! I probably could have done it alone. In fact, I almost did."

Of course, he didn't say that. He gave credit to his teammates—Scottie Pippin, Dennis Rodman, and all the rest. He acknowledged his great coach, Phil Jackson. He even gave credit to the fans.

Michael Jordan expected to be a champion, and he felt free to share credit with others, because he knew that what happened once would happen again (and his team did in fact go on to win a sixth title).

Leaders inspire others with their optimistic view of success. They cast the vision for their driving purpose and then eagerly share credit for its accomplishment with everyone on the team.

After Jesus sent out the seventy-two to perform miracles and preach the Good News, they came back filled with joy and said, "Lord, even the demons submit to us in your name."[12] Jesus affirmed their success and offered a prayer celebrating the work God had done through them. He then told his disciples, "Blessed are the eyes that see what you see. For I tell you that many prophets and kings wanted to see what you see but did not see it, and to hear what you hear but did not hear it."[13]

Make no mistake about it, Jesus was the leader, the source of power for everything his followers did. But he celebrated *their* victory. His success was theirs—and their success was his. As the leader he rejoiced when his team reported that they had taken a step forward in their quest to bring their driving purpose into reality.

Inspirational leaders inspire others with an optimistic view of success. Yet, at the same time they also have an optimistic view of challenges.

An Optimistic View of Challenges

LEMONS, OR LEMONADE?

There are certain sayings that have been quoted so frequently we no longer listen to them. That's unfortunate when you stop to think of it, because some of them are well worth contemplating. For example: "Losers see obstacles where winners see opportunities"; or "Losers see lemons and winners see lemonade."

Nothing characterizes inspirational leaders more than their ability to see the potential hidden in every challenge. Remember the law of success? It says, "Failure is the seed of success." Jesus gave voice to that law and consistently demonstrated his belief in it.

Consider the fact that history's greatest leader recruited ordinary, everyday men with unimpressive résumés—men who were impatient and jealous, men he was training to spread the gospel to the entire world. Developing them into leaders would be like transforming a twenty-two shell into a forty-five magnum. Yet, Jesus never viewed the weaknesses and limitations of his disciples as an obstacle that would prevent the realization of his dream. Instead, he saw their promise, their potential, and he developed it.

Nothing characterizes inspirational leaders more than their ability to see the potential hidden in every challenge.

There were many other challenges Jesus encountered boldly and with unwavering optimism. He faced the temptation of Satan in the desert ... the unbelief of the religious leaders ... the doubt of John the Baptist ... the disease and death of friends ... his impending betrayal, arrest, trial, and crucifixion. In the face of these challenges Jesus always communicated confidence in his ultimate victory and the victory of God's work on behalf of his people.

The 104-Year-Old Optimist

Walt Jones of Tacoma, Washington, illustrates the kind of optimism every leader needs. After his wife of fifty-two years died, 104-year-old Walt bought a motor home in 1976. His wife had only been buried for six months when he was seen driving down the street with an attractive sixty-two-year-old woman at his side. When asked who she was, Walt reported she was his lady friend.

At 104 years of age, Walt Jones was optimistic about more than his romantic life. Two years later, in 1978, with double-

digit inflation heating up the economy, he invested in a con-
dominium development. When asked why, he said, "Ain't you
heard? These are inflationary times. You've got to put your
money into real property so it will appreciate and be around for
your later years when you need it."

In 1980 Walt sold off most of his property in and around
Pierce County, Washington. Because his friends thought he was
cashing in his chips, he gathered them together and told them
he was selling off the property for cash flow: "I took a small
down and a 30-year contract. I got four grand a month comin'
in until I'm 138."[14]

Walt Jones had lived for over a century, and he was still an
optimist ... still growing and looking forward to new challenges. As a leader it's highly unlikely you've got the "handi-
caps" of a 104-year-old man. If he could be optimistic about his
future, so can you. And your optimistic attitude will inspire
those you lead. They'll begin to believe that there is nothing
that can stand between them and the realization of their vision.

PRINCIPLE THREE:

INSPIRATIONAL LEADERS ARE PREPARED

Of course, if all a leader does is stay focused and optimistic,
he or she will have no more substance than a jellyfish. What
often sets inspirational leaders apart is their attention to detail.
Their intense willingness to prepare themselves and their team
for efficient and effective action boosts confidence and
strengthens resolve.

During the years he coached the Los Angeles Lakers to
back-to-back National Basketball Association titles, Pat Riley
realized that if the Lakers were going to win a championship
they would need more than an optimistic vision. After all,
every team dreamed of winning it all. He knew the Lakers
would have to be better prepared than any other team in the
league.

Career-Best Effort

In order to achieve that goal, Riley instituted a program called *Career-Best Effort*—a system aimed at replacing complacency with competency. Each player was ranked against a player from an opposing team. From the five starters to the player sitting on the end of the bench, every player had a category where he could rank number one in the NBA. The idea was for every player to improve in five critical areas of their game over the course of the year. If the program worked, and it proved to do so, the collective effort would be a significant improvement for the entire team.

Effective leaders inspire others by raising the bar of preparation.

Were the Lakers prepared? The record speaks for itself. They won the majority of their games—not only because they had great players but also because those players prepared in such a way that they were able to perform at their peak.

Effective leaders inspire others by raising the bar of preparation. People want to follow a leader whom they know has the ability to bring out the best in them. They eagerly own a vision when they believe that their leader will prepare them to be successful.

Jesus Did His Homework

When it came to preparation, Jesus left nothing to chance. Every time his enemies tried to back him into a corner, Jesus asked questions or made statements that enabled him to elude their grasp. When he resisted the temptations of Satan through a precise knowledge of the Old Testament, it was no accident. Jesus had studied the text so well that he knew what it said and how to apply it to real life.[15] As we've already observed, he endured the suffering of the cross because he had prepared himself the night before by spending time in prayer.

In order to inspire others, you too must be prepared. Spend some time in a quiet place where you can ask God for fresh ideas and invigorating dreams. Read books that strengthen your spirit and provide innovative ideas—Herb Kelleher, the founder, chairman, and chief executive officer of Southwest Airlines, reads five to six books a week (he must spend a lot of time flying!). Brainstorm with other leaders to uncover more effective ways of pursuing your vision. Regularly consider how you can more effectively utilize your resources. It's impossible to overstate the inspirational effect your commitment to preparation can have on those you lead.

"Yeah, I Remember!"

I love the story of the elderly couple who lived in the hills of Georgia. One afternoon as they sat on their porch swing the elderly woman said—in a southern drawl—"Homer, do you 'member when you used to hold my hand?"

"I sure do, Louise," he said as he slowly grasped her hand.

"An' Homer, do you 'member when you used to put yer arm around me and squeeze real tight?"

"I sure do, Louise," he said as he lifted his left arm and draped it around her shoulder.

"An' Homer, do you 'member when you used to nibble on my ear?"

"I sure do, Louise," he said as he pushed himself out of the swing and began shuffling into the house.

"Homer, where ya' goin'?" Louise asked.

"I'm goin' inside to get my teeth," he answered between gummed lips.

Now there was a man who knew he had to be prepared in order to get the job done! What was true of Homer in particular is true of inspirational leaders in general. If you want to inspire those you lead to work harder and dream bigger, you must be prepared to lead them. And you must prepare them to carry out their jobs with excellence.

SUMMING IT UP

Do you genuinely desire to inspire those you lead? Are you honestly interested in enabling them to do what they couldn't, or wouldn't, do without your leadership? If so, these principles are crucial to your success.

- *Stay Focused*. Rivet your attention on your vision and help others do the same. Adapt the way you cast the vision by taking into consideration the individuals you lead. Show them how their contribution is essential to the realization of their dream. If they own the vision, they'll be inspired to make it happen.

- *Be Optimistic*. Maintain a positive attitude that genuinely looks for the best in every situation. View breakdowns as opportunities for improvement. Expect success, and when it arrives, be sure to share the limelight with as many people as possible. View challenges as opportunities for growth, not as obstacles that will defeat you.

- *Be Prepared*. Prepare yourself to carry out your duties with excellence, and prepare your team to successfully carry out theirs.

Having begun this chapter by noting that those you lead will lift you to success, let me conclude by reminding you of that truth. Even now, as you hold this book in your hands, there are people waiting for you as a leader to unleash their potential. They're waiting for you to inspire them to greatness. Because the need is so great, and your role so important, be diligent to cultivate these principles and apply them in your life.

∞

THE WISDOM OF JESUS

- Jesus continually reminded his team of their driving purpose.

- Jesus adapted his message to his audience.

- Jesus viewed life optimistically because he knew his team would win.

- Jesus viewed the failure of his followers as an opportunity for growth.

- Jesus shared the limelight with his followers.

- Jesus viewed obstacles as opportunities.

- Jesus did his homework.

9

FLESH OUT YOUR VALUES

*N*ever was a military decision more important. Thousands of lives and the very outcome of World War II were hanging in the balance. A single man would make the call. In doing so he would prove the validity of Wilfred A. Peterson's words: "Decision is the spark that ignites action. Until a decision is made, nothing happens." After evaluating the weather forecasts and receiving input from his high officials, Gen. Dwight D. Eisenhower gave the order: "Let 'er rip." That single command launched the largest invasion in military history and sent thousands of men to their deaths. It also signaled the end of Nazi Germany.[1]

General Eisenhower was a great military leader not only because he made tough decisions, but also because he made good ones. While it is highly unlikely that you and I will ever be called on to make such an historical decision, we will be expected to make tough calls. We may well be tapped to make decisions about where our church or business will direct its money and its people resources. We may have to determine whether or not an employee gets a promotion or a pink slip.

Occasionally we will have to make the decision alone—and it could well be a difficult decision because lives will be affected and the future of the organization we lead put at risk.

As we look at the example of Jesus, we find three principles of decision making that won't remove the necessity of making tough decisions but will better equip us to make them.

DECISIONS MUST EXPRESS YOUR CORE VALUES

Every time Jesus made a decision it was an expression of his core values: To love God and to love his neighbor. Those two values served as an internal map that guided *every* decision he made. The same should be true of all leaders. Unfortunately, all too often it's not.

Money-Driven Decisions

Unlike Jesus, we can easily get distracted by less important things. We can talk pretty impressively about loving God and other people. But all too often we're swept away by the powerful undercurrent of money, and the possessions, power, and prestige it offers.

Knowing how powerful the lure of money is, Jesus spoke about money more frequently than any other subject except the

> *Every time Jesus made a decision it was an expression of his core values: To love God and to love his neighbor.*

kingdom of God—and he addressed the subject with boldness. Remember, Jesus said we "cannot serve both God and Money."[2] One or the other will become our master. Decisions will be driven either by a desire to acquire wealth, or by a desire to please God. We can't have it both ways.

The words of Jesus frighten me. As a leader I find myself concerned with having enough money to meet budget demands, build facilities, expand ministry programs, and meet the needs of my staff. On a personal level I want to live well and take good care of my family. Actually, that last statement wasn't completely true. I want to live royally. I desire the respect and the influence that wealth offers me. I'm not proud of these dark appetites, but I recognize their existence.

That blend of ministry needs and personal desires creates a setting where I'm tempted to make decisions based on financial considerations rather than on core values. I think the danger is even greater than that. I'm faced with the temptation to allow the acquisition of wealth to *become* a core value, thereby crowding out a love for God and for other people. If that happens, my decisions will be driven by a desire for money rather than by a desire to please God and to live by my core values.

> *Decisions driven by greed and a desire to acquire wealth will eventually lead to the abandonment of our core values.*

What about you? As a leader do you let your desire for money dictate your decisions? If you had to make a decision that would increase profits but violate a core value, what would you do?

Decisions driven by greed and a desire to acquire wealth will eventually lead to the abandonment of our core values. The life of Jesus serves as an exemplary model to keep us from turning away from those values. But there's yet another temptation that will threaten our ability to make leadership decisions based on core values.

Family-Driven Decisions

On the surface it seems as though leadership decisions based on what we believe is best for the family would always be wise decisions. Such may not be the case, however. Consider the time a man came to Jesus and said he would follow him, but first he had to go home and bury his father. Now instead of affirming the man's strong commitment to his family, Jesus said, "Follow me, and let the dead bury their own dead."[3] If I had been that man, I surely would have done a double take and sputtered out something like this to Jesus: "Did I hear you right, Jesus? Did you just tell me to forget about my father, and follow you?"

Of course Jesus knew that the man's father wasn't dead yet. If he had been, custom would have demanded that the man stay with his grieving family. The man wanted to return to his living father and remain with him until his death. He was placing a higher value on his father than on following Jesus.

Contrast that scene with the one described by Luke in which someone told Jesus that his mother and brothers were waiting outside to see him.[4] Instead of dropping everything and hurrying outside to see them, Jesus declared, "My mother and brothers are those who hear God's word and put it into practice."[5]

Jesus' core value of love for God was of supreme significance, taking precedence over one's relationship to one's family. Jesus made it clear that his true family members are those who come to him in faith, those whose first allegiance is to do the will of God.

Among my personal core values is a commitment to deal honestly with family, friends, and business associates. Several years ago I made a commitment to be a keynote speaker at a banquet. A month or so after the engagement had been accepted, a friend offered to fly me to Chicago to watch my oldest son play in a collegiate soccer game.

I was jazzed until I realized the game was on the same day as my speaking engagement in Portland. As I pondered my dilemma I figured the banquet host would understand my desire to bow out of my obligation to his banquet in order to watch my son play in a key game. When I called him on the phone, he expressed disappointment, but he was sympathetic to my situation and released me from my commitment.

Within moments of hanging up the phone I realized I had compromised my core value of honesty for the sake of my son, and my own sake of course. Without delay I called the banquet host back, apologized, and assured him that I would keep my original promise.

In the long run it can hurt our family if we consistently place our allegiance to them above our allegiance to God. The only way our children can learn there are principles of life that take precedence over money and family is to see it incarnated in their parents. If we model a halfhearted commitment to God and a fuzzy approach to truth, then our children will very likely never possess the internal strength required to form and flesh out their own core values. The same is true of all those we lead.

Decisions based on core values will benefit our family over the long haul.

Decisions based on core values will benefit our family over the long haul. As they see these decisions made, our children will learn to utilize a moral compass rather than to rely on personal preferences in making decisions. In the process we'll also be teaching them how to follow in the footsteps of Jesus.

Politically Driven Decisions

The problem for leaders isn't so much identifying the best decision as it is having the courage to carry it out in the face of opposition. Each of us has a tendency to make decisions that are popular . . . decisions that add coins to our political piggy bank.

Not so with Jesus. He made decisions that were founded on his core values, regardless of whomever might be offended. Matthew tells the story of the healing of a demon-possessed man who was blind and mute. Instead of embracing Jesus as the promised Messiah, the religious leaders accused him of performing miracles in the power of Beelzebub, the prince of demons.[6] Did Jesus apologize or back off as a result of their accusations? No way! While his miracles and teachings were like a reoccurring migraine headache to the religious aristocracy, Jesus would not alter his behavior to give them relief. Why? Because he always made decisions that expressed and incarnated his values.

Can you imagine Jesus polling the Pharisees to see if they would endorse the Sabbath healing of a man born blind? Or polling the money changers to identify a specific day when he could drive them out of the temple—a day that would be a little less disruptive of their business? Perhaps you wonder whether Jesus should have handed out a questionnaire to his disciples to see if they would publicly support him calling the Pharisees "whitewashed tombs."

Each of those decisions was an expression of his love for God and for neighbor. To bow to political pressures would have meant allowing a desire for peaceful relationships and personal popularity to drive his decision making.

I'll never forget listening to C. Everett Koop and Francis Schaeffer speak about their book *Whatever Happened to the Human Race.* The book was written to describe the drift of Western civilization away from moral absolutes. At the time of their presentation in the late 1970s, they warned that because our society had accepted the notion that some lives are unworthy to be lived, it wouldn't be long before not only the lives of the unborn but also the terminally ill would be snuffed out. Twenty years later euthanasia was legalized in the state of Oregon as a means of ending life for the terminally ill.

Because I knew of his integrity and honesty, I was thrilled when Dr. Koop became the United States surgeon general. His commitment to value-driven decisions brought him into conflict with both liberals and conservatives. When he was appointed in 1981, liberals objected to his pro-life views, and conservatives objected to his support of sex education in public schools. While he viewed homosexuality as antifamily, an appraisal that conservatives applauded, he regarded AIDS as a health issue, not a moral one, an assessment that liberals applauded.

Dr. Koop's leadership transformed the office of surgeon general from a toothless rubber-stamping agency to a policy-making advocate for national health care. Throughout his lengthy tenure he strove never to make a decision based on political expediency. He once spoke about his ability to survive in Washington, D.C., without resorting to political solutions for medical and social problems. He said, "I have a sense of right and wrong. A lot of people in this town don't have."[7] I would add that he also possessed the courage to make value-driven decisions rather than politically driven ones. As a result conservatives and liberals alike herald his unique leadership skills and his enduring contribution to the nation's health system.

Right decisions are right—whether they are popular or not.

When you're called on to make an important decision, don't concern yourself with its popularity—that will only muddy the water. Issues of popularity are matters of implementation that should be considered *after* the decision has been made. Right decisions are right—whether they are popular or not.

Determine which option best expresses your core values and those of the organization you lead. Once you've made that determination, "Let 'er rip."

DECISIONS MUST EXPRESS YOUR DRIVING PURPOSE

The second element that influenced Jesus' decision making involved his driving purpose. Every miracle he performed, every word he spoke, and every relationship he developed enabled him to more effectively seek and save the lost. The opposite is also true. Jesus didn't heal every sick person, teach every open mind, or build a friendship with every available person. He specifically did not involve himself in activities that would not support and advance his purpose.

I challenge you to read through at least one of the Gospels (Matthew, Mark, Luke, or John) and evaluate every decision Jesus made in the light of his driving purpose. Notice how relentlessly he kept his purpose before him as he decided who to heal, who to teach, and where to go. Nothing sidetracked him from his driving purpose—and nothing should sidetrack you either.

When Jim Casey started his American Messenger Company in Seattle, his purpose was articulated as follows: "To provide the best service all the time." When a decision had to be made regarding their hours of operation, he decided to stay open all night, seven days a week, even though there were relatively few calls for service at night. He wanted his customers—druggists, hotels, restaurants, and the like—to know that they could depend on his company any hour of the day or night. He viewed every call as special.

Because he believed that the *best service* consisted of many things done well, he insisted that his messengers wear uniforms complete with caps and that their shoes be freshly shined every day. Delivery trucks were washed before starting their rounds.

Casey knew that anybody could deliver packages. But he believed that *quality service* was the one thing his company offered that other delivery companies didn't. In the early days his company handled fifty calls a day, using bicycles as the main means of transportation. Today the company he built— now known as United Parcel Service—ships more than twelve million packages a day. From the earliest days of UPS each employee knew that Jim Casey based every decision—large and small—on whether it would provide customers with better service.

It's crucial for you and those you lead to know your driving purpose and that of your organization, and for you to subordinate every decision to that purpose. If you're anything like me I suspect it's easy to become distracted by things that are less important than your core values and driving purpose, to sometimes allow urgent needs to control decisions more than your core values and driving purpose. But if you want to follow Jesus' example by making leadership decisions that are value-driven and purpose-driven, you'll find the next principle helpful.

DECISIONS MUST BE PRAYER-DRIVEN

If the greatest leader of all time—the only man who was without sin, who never made a bad decision, who lived in per-

It's crucial to know your driving purpose and to subordinate every decision to that purpose.

fect harmony with his Father—if that man needed to discuss decisions with God prior to making them, how could we possibly hope to make wise decisions without spending a lot of time in prayer? The answer is clear: We cannot!

Consider the fact that on the night before choosing his disciples Jesus stayed awake *all* night praying about this crucial decision.[8] Now I could imagine praying about an important decision for an hour or so, but all night? What do you think Jesus said as he talked with his Father? Let's see—he very likely prayed for his future disciples by name. And then he probably prayed for their families. And then he surely would have prayed for their individual needs and adjustments. On and on we could go, but we couldn't come close to making a list that would keep us praying *all* night.

Okay, so you may shrug your shoulders and conclude that whatever Jesus was talking about must have been really interesting—remember he did spend the night praying. You may also conclude that following such an example is beyond you, just like walking on water would be beyond you. But wait a minute! One of Jesus' disciples, Peter by name, *did* walk on water—at least for a few steps.[9] Can we conclude that *Jesus will enable you* to spend as much time as is necessary in prayer so you can make wise decisions?

Maybe the real problem is that it's *hard* for you to spend a lot of time in prayer—I know it's hard for me. Or maybe you just don't want to. Prayer is not an easy thing to commit to do. It requires something that's hard to find in the midst of our busy, frantic lives—a time and a place for solitude. The hard truth is unless we place solitude at the top of our priority list, we won't find it at all. And in the process we'll miss God's guidance, which we so desperately need.

I don't know about you, but I don't particularly like where this line of reasoning is headed. I can see already that if we fail to pray before decisions, we have become faithless fools, trying in our own power to accomplish what *God* alone can do in and through us.

How could we possibly hope to make wise decisions without spending a lot of time in prayer? The answer is clear: We cannot!

We become like a bus driver without a map. Not only might we very well be headed in the wrong direction, we're taking everyone on the bus with us as well.

We find ourselves, as leaders, needing to be led ... needing not only a map, but also a Friend to show the way. The more we know this to be true the more we should be compelled to pray, so we can discuss with God *all* decisions—both large and small.

∞

THE WISDOM OF JESUS

- Jesus made decisions that expressed his core values.

- Jesus never allowed money, family, or politics to dictate a decision.

- Jesus made decisions that expressed his driving purpose.

- Jesus prayed before every decision.

10

DEVELOP *WE-ISM*

Teamwork lies at the heart of what it means to be strong, because through teamwork a force is created that's greater than the sum of its parts.

As a leader you must be able to promote teamwork by blending the talents and strengths of individuals. No matter what *Blow Your Socks Off Vision* has captured your heart, it will only become a reality as you join with others to make it happen. Consequently, it's crucial for you to effectively build and lead a winning team. Regardless of your organization's size and influence—it could be your family or a Fortune 500 company—I'd love to be able to give you the tools needed to strengthen it, to help you cultivate a setting where every member says they're happy to play for you (I use the word *play*, because healthy teams invariably seem to make hard work fun).

GET RID OF *ME-ISM*, CULTIVATE *WE-ISM*

Me-ism is an attitude that says, "*My* desires and needs are more important than those of anyone else." Team members who suffer from *me-ism* hog the ball and typically take low-percentage shots. They love the limelight. They complain when they don't get their way and gloat when they do.

Me-ism would be easy for a leader to deal with were it not so widespread. But like the common cold, we're all exposed to its debilitating power.

WHAT WOULD YOU WISH FOR?

Whenever I think of *me-ism* I recall the story of three men who were stranded on an island in the South Pacific. I never heard how they ended up on the island, but they were there for several years when one of them found an old bottle that had washed up on the beach. He didn't think much about it; lots of stuff—nets, dead fish, trash from ships, and countless other things—washed up on the beaches of the island. But this bottle was different, because it was large and black, and it looked very old.

Anyway, he picked up the bottle and carried it back to his friends, who decided to uncork it. There was a loud pop when the cork came out, followed by a swooshing sound—like air rushing out of an open valve on a helium tank used to fill birthday balloons. Of course they knew it wasn't helium coming out of the bottle, but little did they expect that in less than five seconds a tiny white cloud would take the shape of a giant genie—eight feet tall and dressed in a white robe and turban.

You must be able to promote teamwork by blending the talents and strengths of individuals.

"I will give each of you one wish," he said in a deep voice that sounded like Charlton Heston.

No sooner had he made the offer than one of the men said, "I want to go home and be with my family in Dallas." In the blink of an eye he disappeared.

"I want to eat a meal in the best restaurant in the world," the second said. An instant later he too vanished.

The third man looked around at the shack they had built, the beach on which they had spent so much time—and suddenly he felt a sense of total isolation and utter loneliness. In a whisper he said, "I want my friends back."

Me-ism says, "Me first." It is the opposite of *we-ism*, which says, "Team first."

THE DANGER OF *ME-ISM*

The danger of *me-ism* was so great that Jesus refused to tolerate it on his team for even a moment. When the mother of Zebedee's sons, James and John, asked Jesus if he would grant her sons positions of authority in his kingdom, Jesus made it clear that greatness in his kingdom involved *serving*—not being served.[1]

> *Me-ism says, "Me first." It is the opposite of we-ism, which says, "Team first."*

On the night before his crucifixion Jesus prayed for his future disciples—you and me. He could have prayed that we would be strong in spirit or clear in our presentation of the gospel. Instead, Jesus said, "I pray also for those who will believe in me through their message, that all of them may be one."[2] He prayed that we would be united—as a team.

A moment later he prayed a petition that clarified what he had just said. He requested "that they may be one as we are one: I in them and you in me. May they be brought to complete unity to let the world know that you sent me and have loved them even as you have loved me."[3] Jesus prayed that we would experience *we-ism* at the spiritual level with each other and with the triune God.

THE SUPERNATURAL SOURCE OF *WE-ISM*

While I don't understand how God can be one while existing as three distinct persons, I do understand that the Trinity exists as a perfect team. Each member knows his role, and together they are one. While we frail, mortal human beings cannot experience such perfect unity, it's the standard we're to strive for.

Whenever a team is pulling together, we say, "They've really got spirit." That sense of unity is a taste of what God wants to give every team. What I want to establish is that the whole idea of a team flows from the very nature of God. The Father, Son, and Holy Spirit all work together in harmony. I think our desire to experience "teamwork" is evidence of the fact that we bear God's image.

> *The whole idea of a team flows from the very nature of God. The Father, Son, and Holy Spirit all work together in harmony.*

And he alone is able to help us relate to him and to one another as the members of the Trinity relate to one another.

We-ism isn't something that happens naturally. If truth be told, we're all a little like the men on the island, or like James and John—more concerned with ourselves than with others. That's why we must carry out servant leadership (look for more on servant leadership in chapter 13) and be ready to ask God to help our team lay aside personal agendas for the sake of the team and the dream the team is pursuing.

KEEP CASTING THE VISION

Because the vision is the reason the team exists, you must repeatedly urge those you lead to look through the telescope of their imagination and see what it is you're heading for. Jesus himself continually reminded his disciples that they were to stay focused on the task of fishing for people, because their efforts would contribute to the building of God's kingdom.

Jesus never let his followers lose sight of that vision. One of the most compelling examples occurred on the Mount of Transfiguration. After predicting his death Jesus said, "I tell you the truth, some who are standing here will not taste death before they see the Son of Man coming in his kingdom."[4] Now that's a powerful statement that would have stoked the visionary fires of even the most discouraged follower!

Jesus kept the promise six days later when he took Peter, James, and John with him to a high mountain. In that secluded spot Jesus was transfigured before them. Matthew says, "His face shone like the sun, and his clothes became as white as the light."[5] Jesus pulled back the cloak of his humanity and allowed these three men to see his divinity. In doing so he offered them a glimpse of the glory of the coming kingdom. He gave them a taste of what the future held for them. News of the transfiguration must have spread faster than a brush fire, igniting the vision of every follower who heard about it.

A compelling vision has the power to liberate us from me-ism and lead us to we-ism.

All of us want our lives to matter. We want to be a part of something greater than ourselves. That's why a compelling vision has the power to liberate us from *me-ism* and lead us to *we-ism*. It's only as we pull together that we can accomplish something as weighty as the vision to which we've committed our lives.

Everyone's an Eagle

A story is told about a Native American warrior who found an eagle's egg and placed it into the nest of a prairie chicken. The eaglet hatched with the brood of chicks and grew up with them.

Because he thought he was a prairie chicken, the eagle acted like one. He scratched in the dirt for seeds and insects to eat. He clucked and cackled. And he flew in a brief thrashing of wings and a flurry of feathers for only a few feet.

One day the changeling eagle saw a magnificent bird far above him in the cloudless sky. Hanging with graceful majesty on the powerful wind currents, it soared with scarcely a beat of its strong golden wings.

"What a magnificent bird!" the changeling eagle said to a friend. "What is it?"

"That's an eagle—the chief of the birds," his friend replied. "But don't give it a second thought. You could never be like him."

So the young eagle never gave it another thought.

How sad. That bird was created to soar into the heavens but had been conditioned to walk on the ground. With just a touch of vision from a friend that eagle could have realized his potential.

Right now there are people on your team who are thinking like that eagle. They've been created by God to fulfill a great purpose and called to be part of a team that can pull it off. But instead of working with the team, they're living like a prairie chicken—scratching the ground in an isolated corner. They're settling for less than the best, because they're listening to the voices that tell them they could never soar with the eagles. They need you to lead them out of that mind-set by reminding them of their high calling and the *Blow Your Socks Off Vision* they can help make a reality if they apply the principles of *we-ism*.

Because we're all selfish by nature (I've had several people debate that point, but I typically win the argument when I say, "If you're unselfish by nature that means you would have to work hard at being selfish, impatient, and demanding, while patience and sacrifice would come naturally"), and we're all selfish by practice (but don't interpret that to mean we act as selfishly as we could), it's hard to let go of *me-ism*. That's why you must never stop pointing at the eagle in the sky and reminding others of the future in store for them if they put the team first.

Everyone Needs a Reminder

Several years ago I sensed that the congregation I served as pastor was losing enthusiasm for the vision of influencing the greater Portland area for Jesus. We had been meeting in a rented facility for several years while we made plans for a new building and sought God's timing for raising the money needed to build it. While I repeatedly cast the vision not for a building but for touching lives for eternity, I sensed that the church needed a shot in the arm—something to remind them they were destined for something great.

In order to vividly recast the vision in a fresh and creative way, we held a Sunday morning service on the site of the new building. We set up a stage, secured a ring of helium balloons around the property line, and served hot dogs and hamburgers for lunch. Most of the church attendees had never set foot on the property, so nearly everyone showed up.

> *People will make great sacrifices when they believe that their efforts will enable a team to accomplish something extraordinary.*

As I reviewed the interviews videotaped during the celebration, I noticed that the single statement people repeated more than any other was this: "I've never been part of a church with such a great vision." What an exhilarating infusion of energy for moving forward!

Keep casting the vision and challenging your team to unite so the dream can become a reality. There may come a time when you'll need to take your *Blow Your Socks Off Vision* and shape it in such a way that it communicates afresh and motivates your team to a new level of enthusiasm and commitment. As you encourage your team to unite around the vision, there's yet another ingredient that will have to be present. It's an ingredient that builds on this reality: People will make great sacrifices when they believe that their efforts will enable a team to accomplish something extraordinary.

EXPECT SACRIFICE

We-ism develops a strong root system in the soil of sacrifice. The most difficult thing for many people to do as part of a team is to sacrifice—to give of themselves to another person, to the rest of the team. To do so demands giving up immediate personal comfort, ease, recognition, and rewards so that the team will benefit and grow stronger.

Great leaders know that without sacrifice they haven't got a team at all; they've simply got a collection of individuals who occupy the same space at the same time. Such groupings are more like competing bumper cars than a formation of fighter jets.

Jesus, Sacrifice, and We-ism

Sometimes leaders hesitate to call their team to sacrifice. Jesus never demonstrated such reluctance. Consider the day he gathered the Twelve and engaged in a dialogue with them that went something like this (very roughly paraphrased, of course, from Mark 6:7–12):

"I'm sending you out in pairs to the area villages."

"Okay," they said. "We're ready to go."

"You'll need traveling instructions," he said.

"Right!" they replied with pen and pad in hand.

"Take nothing with you except your walking stick."

"Nothing? Surely you must mean we're to travel light. A single carry-on, maybe—you know, the kind that holds a suit, two pairs of pants, three shirts, and the necessary underwear."

"No," Jesus said. "I mean take no money, no bag, and no food. Wear only the clothes on your back and the sandals on your feet."

"That's all?"

"That's all," Jesus replied. "And by the way, you can forget about reserving a room at Motel Six or the Sheraton. You're at the mercy of the villagers."

What's fascinating about the true biblical account (at least it's fascinating to me!) is that there is no record whatsoever that the disciples tried to negotiate a more comfortable travel routine. Mark just notes Jesus' instructions, and then in the next paragraph he tells us that they went out and preached, drove out demons, and healed sick people.

It's easy to breeze over that last thought too quickly. God did great things through these two-man teams *because* they were willing to sacrifice. It doesn't take an astrophysicist to figure out that their mutual sacrifice drew the teams closer together—that it created *we-ism*. And what's more, they began to learn to look to God and to depend on him for whatever results *he* wanted to produce.

SACRIFICE BUILDS LOVE

Many months ago the leadership team at our church realized we needed someone to fill a major hole on our staff team. The more we prayed about it the more we believed that this hole was shaped exactly like Dave Carr—a longtime friend and gifted administrator who shares the core values and driving purpose of the church.

After abundant prayer we approached Dave and offered him a job that would utilize his special abilities in the ministry. Now, you see, Dave already had a good job that provided him with financial security and the promise of upward mobility (Dave is so gifted in his field of expertise that when he received his master's degree he was rated number one in his class and nominated as the top student in the United States).

I figured there was no way a sane person would make a career move that involved abandoning his chosen field of training and taking a cut in pay to boot. Every other member of the core team said, "He has to—the hole fits him!"

Of course, Dave *is* a sane person (who at times has the nerve to question *my* sanity), and yet he did quit his job and join our team. Why? Because he wanted his life to make a difference, and the *Blow Your Socks Off Vision* of the church captured his heart and his imagination.

I never hesitated to ask Dave for sacrifice, because I knew that without a commitment to sacrifice he couldn't be a part of our team. Every one of us has given up something to serve at South Hills. Our willingness to sacrifice is like the binding of a book that keeps the pages together. It's a common touch point that creates respect and builds love. I mean it. I love Dave Carr, and his willingness to give up so much to be a part of the team I lead makes me love him more.

STRIVE FOR EXCELLENCE

It surprised me a number of years ago when I discovered that the single most important ingredient of a winning team is a high standard of performance. I thought it might be prepa-

ration or rewards—which both rank high on the list of significant factors. But research indicates that people do their best when they're challenged to reach beyond what are often self-imposed limits on their achievement standards.

The single most important ingredient of a winning team is a high standard of performance.

That discovery prompted me to consider what Jesus did to raise the bar for his disciples. Of course, Jesus always served up "the best wine." He taught with insight, healed with power, and finished what he started. Jesus did everything with excellence. But of all the things he did to help his team achieve high levels of excellence, two in partic-ular stand out.

Hold People Accountable

"DON'T BE CAUGHT NAPPING . . . I'M COMING BACK!"

Near the end of his earthly ministry, while sitting on the Mount of Olives, Jesus addressed his disciples about his second coming.[6] In a short time Jesus would be gone and his disciples would be responsible to carry on the mission. Without being physically present to teach and encourage them, Jesus knew they could easily slack off—like students when a teacher leaves the classroom. In order to ensure a continuing high stan-dard of performance, Jesus said, in essence, "I'm coming back when you least expect it—so always be ready for my return."

Whenever Jesus used several illustrations to drive home a point, he was helping his listeners see the truth from different angles in order to better understand it. Given that fact, he must have felt this was an especially crucial point, one we would find distinctively difficult to grasp. Notice how repeatedly he hammered home his teaching.

Jesus said his return would be like:

- the great flood in Noah's day—sudden and unexpected.

- robbers who break in when you're not looking for them.

- a homeowner who unexpectedly returns from a trip and inspects his servant's work.

- a wedding in which only the prepared will be allowed to enter.

- a master who returns without warning and demands a profit on his investment.

I find it impossible to read Jesus' warnings and exhortations[7] without a feeling of urgency—or maybe *fear* would better describe my feelings. I don't mean the fear of an abused child who trembles at the thought of his father coming home; I mean the fear associated with knowing that a favorite teacher, coach, or mentor may unexpectedly read with a highly critical eye something I've written. I want to do my best so they'll be pleased with the time they invested in helping me grow.

Nearly two thousand years after Jesus spoke those words I can't help but pause and examine my life. I wonder, "What can I do to be prepared for his return? Will I show a profit on what he's invested in me?" His words have a profound effect on me. When I take them to heart (which I want to do more often), I find myself striving to meet a higher moral standard. I sense a calling to use my time and talents more wisely because I know he will hold me accountable.

For those of us who are leaders his words should prompt us to challenge those under our charge to always give their best effort—regardless of whether they think someone's watching.

They need to know that God will one day ask them to give an account for their life—and that we will hold them accountable right now for how faithfully and skillfully they fill their role on the team.

If this isn't something you're doing at present, I'd suggest you meet with your key players and develop an accountability plan geared to raise the level of their performance. At South Hills we maintain a consistently high standard of programming on Sunday mornings by discussing the various aspects of each service to see how we can make improvements for future services. In fact, we try to analyze every important event to determine the quality and how well it helped us realize our driving purpose. We help teams develop annual strategies, and then we evaluate how effective those strategies are proving to be. On a personal level I consistently seek coaching tips after Sunday morning messages and business seminar presentations.

> *Accountability strengthens a team by identifying members who aren't carrying their share of the load and by rewarding those who are.*

For some people the thought of such accountability may create a paralyzing fear of failure. Gripped by fear they become like the servant who buried his talent because he was afraid he might lose it.[8] This poor guy was so afraid of incurring his master's wrath that he didn't even put the money in the bank where it could have earned interest.

It's important to note that Jesus didn't condemn the master for holding the servant accountable. On the contrary, he faulted the servant for his wicked, lazy heart. Accountability strengthens a team by identifying members who aren't carrying their share of the load and by rewarding those who are.

Regardless of the method you use to hold yourself and others accountable, if you're going to follow the example of Jesus you must do *something* particularly well suited for your team. But as you practice accountability you must carry out yet another practice that will help your team achieve excellence.

Allow People to Fail

As demanding as Jesus was, he repeatedly allowed his team to fail. Consider Peter, who walked on water until he took his eyes off Jesus and took a bath.[9] We already noted the time Jesus instructed his disciples to feed five thousand people with seven loaves and two fish.[10] It only took a moment for them to realize this was an order their sandwich stand couldn't fill. On another occasion they tried unsuccessfully to drive out an evil spirit.[11] And of course there is the story of Peter's repeated denial[12] and the desertion of Jesus by his disciples.[13]

In spite of all these failures, and many others, Jesus never lost confidence in his men. One of the most powerful leadership lessons Jesus exemplified was the creation of a team environment where failure was routine. Excellence and failure are partners, not enemies. In fact, the only way to achieve excellence is through repeated failures. Remember: *Failure is the seed of success.*

"YOU FORGOT YOUR CHANGE!"

Every star basketball player misses shots. Every great receiver drops touchdown passes. Every home run hitter strikes out. Charles Goodyear failed for years and suffered extreme poverty before finally discovering the process for vulcanizing rubber.

During my five-and-a-half years at the University of Texas (all of those language courses took its toll), I worked as a waiter at a Steak 'N Ale restaurant in Austin. One night I served a table of twenty people. The party required nearly constant attention for almost three hours. Of course, I was eager to give the extra attention because I expected a big tip.

When the group left, I found less than a dollar on the tip tray. Instead of pocketing the money and forgetting about it, I clenched my fist around the change, walked over to the side door, and threw the money at the group as they departed. "You forgot your change!" I yelled at them as they walked away under a shower of coins.

Needless to say, these folks weren't too happy with my response to their tip. They stomped back into the restaurant and demanded to talk with the manager, Roy Nunis. Roy patiently listened to their complaint and managed to calm them down. Before they left he gave each of them a certificate for a free dinner.

Even though I had worked for Roy for three years, I thought he was going to fire me right there on the spot. Instead, he sat me down and asked, "Do you want to continue working here?"

I assured him I did.

"Then you'll have to do two things," he told me. "You'll have to paint the fence behind the restaurant, and you'll have to work as a busboy for two weeks."

Roy could have fired me and used my behavior as an example

> *Where there is love there is a freedom to fail—and where there is a freedom to fail you have a setting where new and better ways of doing things will thrive.*

of how *not* to treat customers. Instead, he treated me like a son. Not only did I work there for two more years, I also learned a lesson that has stayed with me for the rest of my life. I discovered the power of accountability wedded with love. In that moment I believe Roy treated me like Jesus would have. By allowing me to fail without provoking my immediate dismissal, he cultivated in me a deeper commitment to him and to the rest of the service team. That event created *we-ism* in me and taught me that love has the power to transform a person and a team.

ACCOUNTABILITY IS SPELLED L-O-V-E

As you strive for excellence, remember to spell accountability *L-O-V-E*. Never forget that where there is love there is a freedom to fail—and where there is a freedom to fail you have a setting where new and better ways of doing things will thrive.

But be on your guard: It's also a setting where conflict can brew and begin to threaten the unity of the team, to dim the vision, and to draw away the resources. In the next chapter we'll examine how the wisdom of Jesus can help you manage conflict and even use it as an impetus for growth.

∞

THE WISDOM OF JESUS

- Jesus did not tolerate *me-ism* on his team.

- Jesus knew *we-ism* found its source in God.

- Jesus helped every member of his team realize his or her potential.

- Jesus expected sacrifice from his team.

- Jesus knew sacrifice flowed from love.

- Jesus held his team to a high standard of excellence.

- Jesus held his team accountable.

- Jesus allowed his team members to fail.

11

KEEP THE TEAM UNITED

The National Institute of Mental Health performed an unusual and fascinating experiment a number of years ago.[1] The experiment took place in a nine-foot cage designed to comfortably house 160 mice. For two and a half years, the colony of mice grew from eight to twenty-two hundred. Plenty of food, water, and other resources were continually provided, and all mortality factors (except aging) were eliminated. Dr. John Calhoun, a research psychologist, began to witness a series of unusual phenomena among the mice as the population reached its peak. Within the cage, from which the mice could not escape, the colony began to disintegrate. Here's what he observed:

- Adults formed groups or cliques of about a dozen mice in each group.

- In those groups different mice performed different social functions.

- The males, who normally protected their territory, withdrew from leadership and became uncharacteristically passive.

- The females became unusually aggressive and forced out the young.

- The whole "mouse society" became disrupted, and after five years "every mouse had died," even though there was an abundance of food, water, and resources, and an absence of disease.

What most impressed the researchers was the strong independence and isolation of the mice. When I read about such research, I realized how much we have become like that "mouse society." We are surrounded by crowds of people, yet we feel isolated. Independence and self-preservation take precedence over compassion, sharing, and caring. Even on teams we can become like passengers on an elevator—heading in the same direction without any personal interaction.

This extreme isolation undermines the ability of teams to interact effectively and accentuates the volatility of conflict. Rather than forcing themselves to work through a relational or philosophical disagreement, team members may withdraw like a spider only to strike out later. Or they may explode like a booby trap, hurling emotional shrapnel at everyone unlucky enough to be nearby.

Because most leaders lack training in conflict resolution, they often feel as helpless as someone trying to sew together a torn garment without needle and thread. They see the tear, but they just don't have the tools to fix it. The situation is even worse for those leaders who may prefer isolation to confrontation. It's a lot easier to dismiss conflict as something that will just go away if it's ignored. Others may prefer to get rid of the source of the conflict by removing the people involved (I had one business leader tell me he never fired anyone—he just made their life so miserable they chose to quit).

Such a passive attitude reflects a weak leadership style that will undermine the unity of the team and cripple its ability to realize the vision. Skilled leaders know how to manage conflict in such a way that it actually strengthens the team and facilitates creativity and growth. If you are a leader, then you realize that conflict is not so much an occasional speed bump as it is the intermittent center-lane stripes

> *Skilled leaders know how to manage conflict in such a way that it actually strengthens the team and facilitates creativity and growth.*

that come in rapid succession. The insights in this chapter contain the potential to strengthen your ability to effectively lead your team because they'll empower you to more skillfully manage conflict. So whether you're seeking to manage a sparring match between two kids, an all-out brawl between two vowed enemies, or a heated debate between two allies, let's look at some principles that can prove helpful.

EMBRACE THE INEVITABILITY OF CONFLICT

Conflict is as unavoidable as traffic in Los Angeles. If you've got two people on a team who never argue, one of them probably isn't needed. Jesus, the greatest leader of all time, experienced conflict among his disciples, between the disciples and himself, and between the religious and political leaders and himself. As long as your team is growing and maturing, there will be conflict. If you refuse to see conflict as an inevitable part of life, you are likely to view it as an unnecessary interruption of the flow—and you may respond to conflict with frustration, anger, and intolerance.

You Control Your Response

Notice that I said "you may respond to conflict." I did not say that "conflict will *make* you respond." The difference is crucial, because in the one case *you* determine your response to a given situation and in the other you become a *victim* of your circumstances. The reality is this: Nobody else has the power to make you angry or frustrated. *You* control your response; other people don't.

> *Nobody else has the power to make you angry or frustrated. You control your response; other people don't.*

I hammered this truth home with my children so effectively that one of them threw it back at me in the heat of an argument. As we verbally sparred over something important (like his responsibility to mow the lawn or fill the car with gas after using it), I could see I wasn't penetrating his defenses. In frustration, I said in a loud and stern voice, "Ryan, you're really making me mad!"

"That's impossible!" he retorted. "*I* can't make you mad—you're responsible for your *own* feelings."

I tried not to laugh, but I couldn't help it. Right in the middle of an argument with my son, I laughed out loud. He had learned the important lessons (okay, maybe he hadn't completely learned them, but at least he had heard them enough times he could repeat them at an appropriate moment) that all leaders need to master if they're going to effectively manage conflict, namely, that *conflict is unavoidable* and that *I determine how I will respond when conflict hits.*

Childhood Lessons on Managing Conflict

As I've coached leaders and families in the management of conflict, I've discovered that most tend to use the conflict resolution skills they learned while growing up. Unfortunately, those skills in many cases reflect the experiences of growing up in a dysfunctional family of origin.

Both my parents engaged in frequent no-holds-barred arguments. What seems odd, as I look back, is that the day after one of those fights my parents *acted* as though nothing had happened. I had to be very careful what I said in the aftermath, because the slightest misspoken word could trigger a fresh argument.

Growing up I learned two lessons from my family—one about *avoiding* conflicts, and the other about *winning* them. I learned to avoid conflicts by saying whatever I thought the listener wanted to hear; truth just wasn't as important to me as peace. Second, if an argument erupted, I learned to win in a conflict by finding someone's vulnerable spot and throwing a verbal blow where it would do the most emotional damage.

As I matured and entered into adult relationships, it didn't take long to discover that my conflict resolution skills were woefully ineffective. While I had a well-honed ability to blow people out of the water with a verbal attack or to pacify them with half-truths, whatever peace I happened to bring about was short-lived.

While your family of origin may not have been *that* dysfunctional (of course, I realize it could have been much worse), chances are the methods of conflict resolution you learned as you grew up weren't a whole lot better. And now when you find yourself or those on your team experiencing conflict, you tend to revert back to what you learned while growing up.

Abandon Ineffective Methods

Can you remember ever telling someone, "You make me so mad!"? When you did so, you were blaming him or her for your reaction and perhaps using one of the ineffective methods of conflict resolution you learned while growing up methods that allowed you to act destructively without assuming responsibility for your actions or that allowed you to tell yourself, "Because this person made me mad, he's to blame for my actions."

While responding in such a way may have brought a sort of balance to your family of origin, it often doesn't work well in other contexts. Consequently, your ways of thinking and acting may be bringing as much peace as a lit match placed on the fuse of a firecracker. As things disintegrate you may be sensing

147

that you're losing control of your reactions—and the situation as well.

The problem is intensified by the fact that as the leader you hold most of the chips. You express your frustration inappropriately—and what can anybody else do? If an angry basketball coach kicks a chair across the court, what can a player do? When chief executive officers verbally blast junior officers, they know they're beyond their subordinates' reach.

> *As we control our response to conflict, we will then be able to coach others through the situation in a constructive way.*

While you may not exhibit those specific behaviors, I suspect you do occasionally use your influence destructively during a conflict.

If you don't always effectively manage *yourself* during a conflict, it makes sense that your confidence level would be low when it comes to refereeing *someone else's* fight.

When we do something often enough a groove is formed, with no visible way out. We call that condition *being in a rut*. Getting out of this rut demands that we acknowledge that conflict is inevitable and that we cultivate the ability to control how we respond to it. As we control our response to conflict, we will then be able to coach others through the situation in a constructive way. Let's draw now on the wisdom of Jesus to discover how we can more effectively manage ourselves during a conflict.

EMBRACE EFFECTIVE METHODS

Be Controlled by God—Not Other People

One of Jesus' most controversial and misunderstood teachings had to do with the subject of forgiveness. In the Old Testament the Hebrew people were commanded to seek equal recompense for a wrong suffered. They were told to take "eye for eye, tooth for tooth, hand for hand, foot for foot."[2] At first blush such a law seems harsh, but it was actually introduced by God to limit retribution. Prior to its institution if someone had lost an eye they might feel justified in killing the man who had maimed them.

While this law had stood for centuries as a way of curbing evil, Jesus didn't hesitate to replace it with a better one. He told his followers, "If someone strikes you on the right cheek, turn to him the other also."[3] I'm of the opinion that Jesus wasn't commanding us to stand still while an opponent beats us to death. Rather, I think he was telling us to never allow someone else's wrath to control our response. Never retaliate in kind. Instead, endure the insult and respond with generosity. Jesus consistently taught that God's kingdom citizens are to be controlled by the heart and mind of the King, not by the wrath of an enemy.

No matter how you interpret Jesus' words, they are undeniably difficult to put into practice. I honestly don't know how I'd respond if someone slapped me on the cheek. I do know I have a hard time demonstrating patience when a wild-eyed driver cuts me off while I'm cruising down the freeway (of course, when *I* cut someone off I'm surely *not* wild-eyed—I just didn't see them!). If patience is hard to practice under that situation, I have a sneaking suspicion it would be even harder if someone slapped me across the cheek.

What's Behind Generosity?

Because Jesus knew his words were hard, he went on to explain how they could be applied in real-life situations. He said, "Love your enemies."[4] Behind generosity is love. Now that's a profound thought, not only because of what it says, but also because of what it doesn't say. If love is behind generosity, then what is behind retaliation? Could it be greed? Or hatred? If so, then the words of Jesus have ripped the mask off our commitment to retaliation and exposed a hate-filled monster lurking in our soul.

I find the words of Jesus troubling because I'd rather not see retaliation in such a bad light. It's a sin I've always been able to

149

justify by telling myself, "I only tailgated that guy because he cut me off back there"; or "Of course I laid on the horn for ten seconds without interruption—he cut me off and needed to be disciplined" (I use that illustration because I suspect you've done the same thing, and besides, I'm too ashamed to mention some of the nastier stuff I've done).

> We must remain consciously connected to God so that when we enter a conflict we can respond with a generosity that's motivated by love.

As usual, Jesus wants to take us a step deeper. That's why he said if we want to be like our Father in heaven we will love our enemies.[5] The progression of Jesus' logic is profound. In essence, Jesus teaches that behind generosity is love, and behind love is God. We can only conclude that if *God* is guiding and controlling our lives, then it must be true that the following people are not:

- those who slander us.

- those who persecute us.

- those who argue with us.

- those who verbally attack us.

- those who threaten to take away all we cherish.

Every time we respond to someone with a retaliatory spirit we become like a fish on a hook—and our opponent is holding the line. Citizens of God's kingdom aren't to allow others to control them; instead, we must respond to others as God would.

God extends kindness even to those who oppose him, because he loves them. Jesus himself teaches that God shows his love to people without distinction: "He [the heavenly Father] causes his sun to rise on the evil and the good, and sends rain on the righteous and the unrighteous."[6] That kind of love without distinction is exactly what you and I must show.

We must remain consciously connected to God so that when we enter a conflict we can respond with a generosity that's motivated by love.

How Can I Love an Enemy?

Such a course of action would be relatively easy if it weren't for one thing—when I'm embroiled in a conflict I don't feel very spiritual. I'm mad (not because somebody made me mad, but because I responded that way!), confused, fearful, or just plain hurt.

As I face these issues in my life, I go back to Jesus' words, where I discover the key to loving an enemy. Jesus urges, "Pray for those who persecute you."[7] The only way I can connect with God *and* love my opponents is if God infuses me with his love and grace. I become like the branch that wants to bear fruit—it must rely on the vine to produce the fruit through it.[8] I feel confident in saying that the most important thing you can do to handle a conflict as Jesus would is to talk the matter over with God.

Below is an illustration that summarizes my view of Jesus' teaching about managing ourselves in the midst of a conflict:

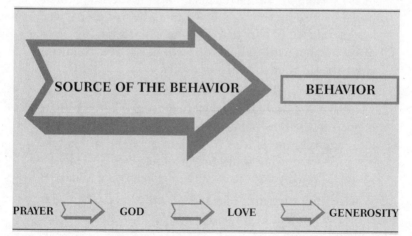

If this sounds oversimplified, let me assure you that it's not easy to put this teaching into practice. Many of us stubbornly resist the act of praying, and our resistance reveals that the biggest enemies we face in a conflict aren't the ones who oppose us, but *our own hearts*. We prefer to arrive at our own solutions without getting direction from God. And when we do, we may speak and act in harmful ways because we have failed to effectively bridle our pride.

"Don't Get Mad. Get Even!"

I find it fascinating that men and women who possess the leadership skills needed to build great companies often lack the ability to work through conflicts in a healthy way. Lee Iacocca is widely recognized as one of the most brilliant business leaders in recent history. His genius lay behind the development of the Ford Mustang, and he later salvaged the Chrysler Corporation. Mr. Iacocca has known great success and has endured great hurt. After thirty-two years with Ford Motor Company he was forced to resign. In his book *Iacocca: An Autobiography*, Mr. Iacocca describes what he believes brought about his forced departure. As you read his words, and the interview that follows, take note of the "eye for eye" mentality:

> In 1975, Henry Ford started his month-by-month premeditated plan to destroy me. Until then, he had pretty well left me alone. But in that year he started having chest pains, and he really didn't look well. It was then that King Henry began to realize his mortality.
>
> He turned animal. I imagine his first impulse was: "I don't want that Italian interloper taking over. What's going to happen to the family business if I get a heart attack and die? Before I know it, he'll sneak in here one night, take my name off the building and turn this place into Iacocca Motor Company. Where does that leave my son, Edsel?"
>
> When Henry thought I'd steal the family jewels, he had to get rid of me. But he didn't have the guts to just go ahead and do his own dirty work. Besides, he knew he'd never get away with it. Instead, he played Machiavelli, determined to humiliate me into quitting.[9]

Several years later, in an interview aired on an NBC television program, *Iacocca: An American Profile,* Iacocca spoke about Henry Ford and vowed: "That's something I won't forgive . . . I told my kids, 'Don't get mad, get even.' . . . I did it in the marketplace. I wounded him badly. It took me five years."

Most leaders can identify with Iacocca. We know the pain of betrayal and rejection. We understand what it's like to have someone want to destroy us. And we know what it's like to withhold forgiveness and crave revenge.

THE HIGH ROAD

Jesus calls us to take another path—a high road. If we're going to follow his example and put into practice his teachings, we will not react to the wrath of an opponent with equal wrath. We will choose to root out pride and bitterness from our heart—by spending as much time in prayer as will soften our heart. We will then be in a position to apply the two most crucial principles of conflict management Jesus gave us.

The single most important principle is by far the hardest to put into practice. I've lost count of the number of times I've seen a disagreement escalate because this step was disregarded.

PRINCIPLE ONE:

IF YOU HAVE A PROBLEM WITH SOMEONE,
MEET WITH HIM OR HER PERSONALLY

Jesus said, "If you are offering your gift at the altar and there remember that your brother has something against you, leave your gift there in front of the altar. First go and be reconciled to your brother."[10] Later he told his disciples, "If a brother sins against you, go and show him his fault, just between the two of you."[11]

I know that these verses deal specifically with the subject of "sins" that people commit against one another, and I am *not* suggesting that whenever two people are in conflict one or the other has sinned. But I *am* insisting that a broader principle can be drawn from Jesus' words—a principle that applies to people who are in conflict: Whenever you have a conflict with someone, meet with him or her personally (privately when it's appropriate and possible) to discuss the situation.

Whenever you have a conflict with someone, meet with him or her personally (privately when it's appropriate and possible) to discuss the situation.

Jesus consistently put this principle into practice. During his temptation he confronted Satan, his greatest enemy.[12] Jesus repeatedly rebuked his disciples for their unbelief and spiritual dullness.[13] When Peter's interests were in conflict with God's, Jesus didn't pull any punches—he told the fisherman, "Get behind me, Satan!"[14] He chided the disciples when they argued about which of them would be greatest in the kingdom of God.[15] And of course, he wasn't reluctant to confront the religious leaders about their hypocrisy.[16]

Jesus taught and modeled the principle of talking personally with those with whom he had a conflict. Following his example doesn't come naturally for most leaders or followers. As a leader you may discover that the last thing a subordinate wants to do is come to you directly to discuss a personal or philosophical disagreement. Numerous times I've heard through a third party about a problem someone had with me. As I met together with that individual and discussed the issue I always asked, "Why didn't you come and talk to me?" Almost without exception they answered, "I was afraid to." Or "I didn't think you'd listen." This response is characteristic of the way many people feel about approaching a leader with a problem—about as safe as a deer when it catches the scent of a hunter!

Initiate Meetings

While you as a leader may have an "open-door policy," your team members may judge that it is a waste of time to tell you something you don't want to hear. To avoid placing this kind of burden of judgment on others, consider the wisdom of initiating meetings where you facilitate an open discussion about how the team is doing, how they personally as team members are doing, and how the two of you are doing. Ask leading questions that allow them to open up—and refrain from passing judgment on what they say so they feel free to honestly express themselves.

Apologize

If someone lets you know you dropped the ball in a given situation, admit it and apologize. Few things communicate a genuine sense of integrity like a heartfelt apology. During a 1775 election campaign for seats in the Virginia assembly, a twenty-three-year-old colonel named George Washington insulted a hot-tempered man named Payne, who immediately knocked Washington down with a hickory stick (Payne presumably used a stick because he was smaller than the nation's founding father). Soldiers rushed to avenge their friend, who got to his feet in time to hold them off, assuring them that he could take care of himself.

> *It's imperative to establish a cultural norm on your team in which everybody knows that disagreements are handled privately, personally, and quickly.*

The next day Washington wrote Payne a letter, asking for a meeting in a tavern. When Payne arrived at the tavern, he expected a demand for an apology and a challenge to a duel. Instead, Washington apologized for the insult that had provoked the blow, expressed his hope that Payne was satisfied, and then offered his hand in friendship.[17]

Strong leaders possess the courage and wisdom to meet personally with someone with whom they're in conflict, and then to apologize whenever necessary. Doing so not only has the power to heal a broken relationship, it encourages other team members to admit their missteps as well.

155

It's imperative to establish a cultural norm on your team in which everybody knows that disagreements are handled privately, personally, and quickly. The longer a disagreement festers the more damage it can cause.

When we refuse to take the initiative for meeting personally with others, it could very well be because we're utilizing the conflict management skills we learned while growing up. Perhaps the time has come for you to toss aside failed practices and begin to put into practice principles that work.

Principle Two:

If You've Been Wronged, Extend Forgiveness

I'm not sure why, but I haven't found it difficult to overlook a wrong committed against me—especially when an apology is extended. (It might be because I have such a lousy memory I forget what happened.) Over the years I've made the unfortunate mistake of assuming that everyone else found it relatively easy to forgive an offense. They don't. Indeed, I've discovered forgiveness doesn't come easily for most people. That's especially true when their sense of justice has been violated. They'll often wonder aloud, "How could he or she do such a thing? I would never do that to anyone!"

An unforgiving attitude is dangerous to a team, because when team members chew on a wrong they've suffered, like a dog gnawing on a bone, they undermine the unity and strength of a team.

If you're going to manage conflict, it's essential for you to forgive wrongs committed against you and to expect the same effort from the rest of your team. Of course, I'm not talking about job performance here. I'm referring to personal offenses that members of your team will commit against one another in the course of working together. These offenses may include an insensitive word, the overstepping of a boundary, a failure to acknowledge the source of a good idea, or a host of other irritants that can eat away at a relationship.

Because dynamic teams are typically made up of people with very different temperaments, these offenses often occur on a regular basis. Jesus certainly had to cope with personality differences among his disciples. Consider the following:

- Peter was an impulsive mover and shaker.

- James was ambitious, short-tempered, politically minded, and judgmental.

- John had a loving heart but was much like his brother, James.

- Andrew (Peter's brother) was a middleman who was approachable and pleasant.

- Matthew was a tough, dishonest "numbers" man with a good mind and a bad reputation.

- Thomas was a pessimistic doubter who lacked vision and possessed courage.

- Philip was a doubter and a questioner.

- Bartholomew was a quiet, studious man with high integrity.

- Judas was a greedy and treacherous administrator.

Talk about diversity! These men must have repeatedly butted heads. They no doubt had plenty of wrongs to overlook—which is probably why they stammered, "Increase our faith!"[18] in response to Jesus' plea that they forgive each other seven times in a single day.

I can just see these guys hearing the words of Jesus, looking at each other, and shaking their heads in disbelief. They must

> *If you're going to manage conflicts, it's essential for you to forgive wrongs committed against you and to expect the same effort from the rest of your team.*

have concluded that there was no way they could follow this

command. But Jesus *knew* they could—and he knows we can too. That's why he told them the issue wasn't one of faith but of obedience—of doing what they were told to do.

After all, Jesus said, "If you have faith as small as a mustard seed, you can say to this mulberry tree, 'Be uprooted and planted in the sea,' and it will obey you."[19]

What a powerful lesson! No matter how deep a root of bitterness may have grown in your heart, God has the power to uproot it. But you must trust him to do so—and so must your fellow team members. Ultimately, an unwillingness to forgive is driven by a spirit of disobedience, not by an actual inability to forgive.

As you and your team members repeatedly forgive those who wrong you, you'll discover a freedom and joy that will unleash creativity and encourage diversity.

VELCRO AND TEFLON

Let me leave you with two visual images that have changed my life.

The first time I saw Velcro, my oldest son had just learned to tie his shoes. No sooner had he mastered that amazing feat of digital dexterity than a friend came over with a brand-spanking-new pair of tennis shoes. His shoes were "laced" (not really laced but secured on his foot) with Velcro straps. I saw him rrrrip off those straps—and my eyes popped open. In a twinkling of an eye he slipped off his shoes.

It was such a novelty to me back then that I knelt down and picked up the shoe and played with the straps for several minutes. Nowadays, of course, all sorts of things are attached with Velcro. In fact, I keep a stash of it around the house just in case I need it.

And then there's Teflon. You know about Teflon. Unlike Velcro—which makes things hold together—Teflon *keeps* things from sticking together when you don't want them to— things like a frying pan and scrambled eggs.

When you think of managing conflict—whether at home or with the team you lead—do yourself, and those you lead, a favor. Remember Velcro and Teflon. Whenever someone wrongs you, you're going to respond as though you had a Teflon coating—you're going to let it slide. And when it comes to those you're in conflict with—you're going to treat them generously, because you're going to cling to God and his love like one piece of Velcro stuck to another.

∞

THE WISDOM OF JESUS

- Jesus responded to insults with generosity.

- Jesus taught his followers to be controlled by God, not by the wrath of an enemy.

- Jesus always responded to conflict with love—even if it was tough love.

- Jesus knew the key to loving an enemy was an intimate connection with God nurtured through prayer.

- Jesus urged his followers to resolve conflicts personally, privately, and quickly.

- Jesus taught his followers to initiate communication with an opponent—regardless of who started the conflict.

- Jesus taught his team to eagerly extend forgiveness.

12

BE A CHANGE MASTER

*T*he world is changing so fast that in the early part of the twenty-first century there will be only two kinds of leaders—"the quick and the dead." MCI's head of development Dick Liebhaber has facetiously observed, "New developments in telecommunications technology seem to come about twice a day." Steven Brull, writing in the *International Herald Tribune*, observed, "Since 1979, when Sony Corp. invented the Walkman, the company has developed 227 different models, or about one every three weeks."[1] What's happening at Sony is happening in companies everywhere. The world is changing!

Meanwhile, the Internet has added warp speed to everything from buying a book to trading commodities, while cell phones have provided instant communication. A few years ago only the rich and powerful were seen talking on a phone while driving their car. Nowadays, teenagers use cell phones to chat with friends and call home. The changes in the world are affecting everyone.

No Such Thing as "Normal"

In the past change was a relatively slow process, like the gradual eroding of the shoreline. When a cycle of change was completed, things settled down to "normal." The world is different now, as author and educator Jeanenne LaMarsh has observed: "Change is a constant; multiple changes happen simultaneously with no 'normal' in sight."[2]

The changes in the world are so widespread and far-reaching that there is virtually no place you can go to get away from them—

> *The changes in the world are so widespread and far-reaching that there is virtually no place you can go to get away from them—there is no island of normalcy.*

there is no island of normalcy. It's an upheaval that comes along once every two hundred years, and there's no sign it's slowing down. Indeed, it only seems to be speeding up, like a video on perpetual fast-forward. As a leader your job is to boldly step into that video and escort your team along with you.

Of course, you've probably already figured out that stepping in is easier than carrying your team along. Regardless of the changes you want to institute, not everyone will automatically follow. You may very well have to invest considerable time and effort to win their support.

Seize the Opportunity

As you contemplate the risks and rewards associated with change, you must beware: You can't sit and wait for change to happen to you and your organization. You must seize the opportunity and bring about the changes *you* want. The great English playwright and poet William Shakespeare wrote of strategic moments that must be grabbed at once:

There is a tide in the affairs of men,
Which, taken at the flood, leads on to fortune;

Omitted, all the voyage of their life
Is bound in shallows and in miseries:
And we must take the current when it serves,
Or lose our ventures.[3]

When the tide is high, we must board the ship and begin the voyage. The tide won't wait—and neither will strategic opportunities to realize positive change. When the circumstances for success merge, you must be the change master. You must lead others into a better tomorrow. You must do for your team what Jesus did for his disciples. You must clear the trail and make it possible for your team to follow. In this chapter we'll present several principles drawn from the life and teachings of Jesus, who instituted the most radical transformation in world history—principles that will enable you to establish a setting where dynamic change is a welcome reality.

PRINCIPLE ONE:

TO CHANGE THE PRESENT, DESCRIBE THE FUTURE

It may surprise you to hear that many of the people you lead think you know exactly what the future looks like. And they may think you're not telling them what it looks like because you're afraid they won't like the future you have planned.

In light of this amazing revelation, here's a bit of wise counsel (at least I hope it's wise!): Tell everyone in the organization where you're going. Repeatedly share the *Blow Your Socks Off Vision*. Fill in as much detail as possible, but be careful to only tell what you know while honestly admitting what you don't know. If the picture is fuzzy, admit it. Tell your team you're unable to fill in the missing pieces or turn the dream into reality without their help.

Jesus the Vision Caster

From the earliest days of his public ministry Jesus described the kingdom of God *and* the role of his followers in that kingdom. The use of the word *and* is important. Not only did his disciples hear what the kingdom would look like, they heard what they would be doing as well. (One of the greatest fears people have of change is fueled by uncertainty about their role in the new order of things brought about by change.)

For a taste of how Jesus accomplished his goal, turn to the Sermon on the Mount.[4] The Beatitudes[5] describe the attitudes of citizens of God's kingdom, and the rest of the message[6] describes their actions. Later, at the Mount of Transfiguration, Peter, James, and John got a first-hand look at the King in his glory—a spectacular, unforgettable glimpse of what is to be fully revealed when Jesus comes again.[7]

You need to repeatedly tell those you lead what the future looks like in your mind's eye.

You need to repeatedly tell those you lead what the future looks like in your mind's eye. Of course, you may be thinking, "But we haven't arrived at a *Blow Your Socks Off Vision* yet." If so, it would be wise for you to begin the process of identifying your core values, driving purpose, and *Blow Your Socks Off Vision*. Involve as many people as possible in the process. Ultimately, any institutional, programmatic, or process change that needs to take place will be a reflection of your core values and driving purpose.

Show How the Changes Support the Vision

Leaders who arrive on the scene and immediately begin to describe the changes they intend to institute will suddenly be faced with the nearly impossible task of rounding up and rallying a group of people who resemble frightened cats. But leaders who arrive at a consensus on the core values, driving purpose, and *Blow Your Socks Off Vision* will find people more inclined to unite around changes that will help bring the vision into reality.

Once the dream has been articulated, it's of the utmost importance to tell people where you're going and to help them see how they fit in. Casting the vision is not a one-shot deal; it's something you must continually carry out (I repeat this time and again, because it's one of your most important jobs as a leader).

Maybe you're thinking, "I've already tried to cast the vision, and it didn't work." Or it could be that you're facing stiff resistance in strategic places that causes you to question whether you can bring about any real change. If so, the next principle will prove helpful.

PRINCIPLE TWO:

TO LOOSEN RESISTANCE, CHALLENGE ASSUMPTIONS

I was surprised to scan a Harris poll that revealed over ninety percent of the people surveyed would change their lives dramatically if they could; moreover, they ranked such intangibles as self-respect, affection, and acceptance higher than status, money, and power.[8] One might naturally conclude that while most people don't like the way they live, they don't know what to do about it. They don't know how to change. Those ninety percent would probably be willing to rally behind a leader who could help them make the changes they hunger for.

But let's not overlook an important element of that poll. When I first read its findings, I said aloud, "What about the other ten percent?" It would be easy to ignore them, because they're such a small minority. And while I don't know what, if anything, Harris found out about them, my instincts tell me that a few of them will go along with a change, some will walk away, and the remaining few will fight like junkyard dogs.

Jesus faced resistance from his disciples (remember Peter saying, "Never, Lord!"[9] after Jesus predicted his own death in Jerusalem), from the people of his hometown (Jesus said, "Only in his hometown, among his relatives and in his own house is a prophet without honor"[10]), from the crowds, and from the religious leaders. His ideas were so revolutionary that insightful people realized that they contained the potential to turn the existing order upside down.

Identify the Assumption and Challenge Its Validity

While repeatedly casting the vision, Jesus routinely challenged people's assumptions. The Pharisees had concluded that because Jesus hung around with sinners, he must be one himself. Their repugnance was based on the assumption that God hated sinners and wanted nothing to do with them. Jesus urged them to think differently when he described God as one who loves sinful people, searches for them, and rejoices when they're found.[11]

When the Pharisees challenged Jesus for allowing his disciples to eat without first washing their hands,[12] they assumed that God cared more about man-made traditions than about the condition of human hearts. That assumption was the basis for an elaborate religious system that allowed the Pharisees to exercise power over people by making sure they conformed to their meticulous rules and regulations.

Jesus never explained why it wasn't a matter of grave concern to him if his disciples ate without first washing their hands; instead, he exposed the weakness of his opponents' assumption by pointing out that they regularly violated *God's command* to honor their parents.[13]

The problem Jesus confronted was one every leader faces. The Pharisees assumed certain things to be true, and based on those assumptions they developed a menu of activities and institutions. In such cases it isn't long before the activities and traditions are believed to be valid—because nobody ever thinks to challenge the assumptions on which they are based. In his thought-provoking book titled *Lateral Thinking*, Edward de Bono points out, "It is historical continuity that maintains most assumptions—not a repeated assessment of their validity."[14]

Rearrange This!

Mr. de Bono illustrates his point by asking the reader to arrange the following shapes into a single shape that would be easy to describe.

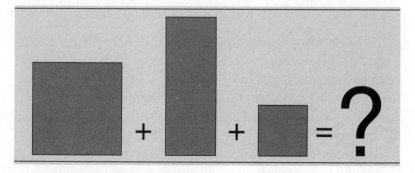

You'll probably agree the problem has no apparent solution. But suppose you weren't limited by the assumption that the shapes can't be altered. If you cut the first one in half, it would be easy to arrange them into a recognizable shape.

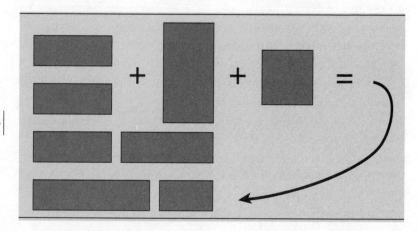

De Bono observes that if you did such a thing people would accuse you of cheating.[15] The problem is that they assumed a certain set of rules—the shapes must remain the same—which makes a solution impossible. Solving the problem involved challenging that assumption.

New Solutions Demand Valid Assumptions

While it's true that there are boundaries that limit how we solve problems, implementing change demands that we challenge assumptions. As a skyscraper needs a stable foundation, so the programs and institutions we develop need valid assumptions to hold them up.

Several years ago I read about a man who was reading a newspaper while riding in a train. He tried to concentrate, but two young children repeatedly interrupted him by running up and down the aisle and slapping their hands on the back of the seats. Meanwhile, their father sat calmly in his seat across from the man, oblivious to all the commotion.

The passenger assumed that the father was a terrible parent. Time and again he lowered his newspaper and shot the man a dirty look, hoping that he'd catch the hint and get his children under control. As the train rolled to a stop and the two men got up to leave, the father looked at the passenger and said, "Please forgive me for not controlling my kids. We buried their mother this morning, and I'm so shocked and exhausted I just don't have the energy to keep them in check."

Implementing change demands that we challenge assumptions.

Everyone Should Ask Why, Why, Why

The annoyed passenger suddenly changed his judgmental attitude because he now understood that his assumption was false. Those you wish to influence need you to question, and oppose where necessary, their individual perceptions and the actions that flow from them. Create the kind of environment where everyone on the team is encouraged to constantly ask why.

"Why do we do things this way?"

"Why can't we do things differently?"

"Why haven't we changed this before?"

"Why do we want to change this now?"

When we ask why, we force ourselves, and those on our team, to challenge our fundamental assumptions.

Jesus realized the danger of making false assumptions and accepting the conclusions that flow from those assumptions. One day his critics asked him why his disciples ate and drank while John's disciples, and those of the Pharisees, fasted and prayed.[16] Jesus answered their question in a way that discloses a third principle crucial to bringing about change.

PRINCIPLE THREE:

TO UNDERMINE ASSUMPTIONS, PAINT VIVID WORD PICTURES

Jesus responded to the challenge by asking a question about a bridegroom: "Can you make the guests of the bridegroom fast while he is with them? But the time will come when the bridegroom will be taken from them; in those days they will fast."[17] Jesus was the bridegroom, and while he was with his disciples it was appropriate for them to celebrate and join in the feast.

But Jesus understood what it was that stood behind the question. He realized that the real issue was the religious leaders' assumption that things should continue to be done as they had always been done—and it was *not* customary for spiritual people to eat and drink, but instead to fast and pray. The religious leaders assumed that their form of religion was the best—and Jesus and everybody else better conform to it—or else! Jesus challenged their assumptions by sharing yet another vivid word picture.

168

New Wine and Old Wineskins

In the Gospel of Luke Jesus declared, "No one pours new wine into old wineskins. If he does, the new wine will burst the skins, the wine will run out and the wineskins will be ruined. No, new wine must be poured into new wineskins."[18]

The rules his critics played by didn't allow for any changes in the existing system. Jesus made it clear that the old system could not contain his message and the growth it would produce. Like Jesus' critics, the people we lead have their established ways of doing things—and they may never have had anyone challenge the assumptions on which their behavior is based. If in the process of examining the assumptions you encounter resistance, bear in mind that analogies are helpful because people identify with them and they touch an emotional chord. After all, many times people *feel* intuitively that something is right long before they mentally process the information.

> *Analogies are helpful because people identify with them and they touch an emotional chord.*

Analogies also allow you to talk about something (the subject of the story) in a way that doesn't threaten the hearers. The story's purpose isn't so much to prove the validity of a particular point of view as to open up the listener to the possibility that a cherished assumption should be reconsidered.

Learn a Lesson from Sherlock Holmes

Suppose you're trying to persuade strategic team members to reevaluate and perhaps rephrase the core values of the organization you've recently begun to lead. (While I noted in chapter 3 that core values never change, they should be regularly examined.)

"We've already done that," someone interjects.

"Besides, core values don't change!" another person points out.

You realize you're dealing with a group of individuals who have assumed that once core values are adopted they're no longer subject to evaluation.

"But what if something was missed?" you ask.

"Couldn't have happened," a third person interjects. "Too much time and effort went into developing them."

You pause for a moment and then say, "I just don't want us to fall into the trap that caught Dr. Watson in one of Sherlock Holmes's cases."

Heads tilt and eyes stare with looks of bewilderment. Finally someone asks, "What do you mean?"

You lean forward in your chair and say, "It was the case where Dr. Watson dismissed a dog as unimportant because it had done nothing on the night of the crime. Mr. Holmes wisely noted that the dog was significant precisely because it had done nothing." Your small audience is unsure where you're headed, but as you hesitate they urge you to finish the story.

You smile and continue, "Sherlock Holmes realized the fact that the dog didn't bark meant the criminal must have known the dog. And that crucial fact narrowed down the list of potential suspects."

Having told the story, you make your point. "I think it's possible, just possible, that something may have been overlooked in the articulation of the core values. I'd like us to consider reviewing them once more to be sure they still represent us—and we represent them."

The purpose of that analogy wasn't to win an argument, but to overcome the resistance of your team to reassess the assumption that established core values shouldn't be reexamined.

When Jesus told the parables of the bridegroom and the new wine in old wineskins, he was inviting his listeners to reevaluate an historical assumption. If they would do that, then they might be open to the radical changes he was introducing to them.

Because people form opinions based on previously held assumptions, and then search for information to validate them, they tend to ignore anything that contradicts their assumptions. Their minds become like radar screens programmed to only identify incoming objects that are friendly.

As a pastor I've lost count of the number of times people have told me, "We've never done it that way before." Of course, in the context of the church, people tend to spiritualize their assumptions and the philosophies, programs, and institutions that flow from them. Consequently, not only do they hold to the traditional way things have been done, they also insist that their viewpoint is actually God's viewpoint—which

Rather than fighting it out at the "OK Corral," it's far better to delay making a judgment until additional questions have been addressed.

means, of course, that if you disagree with them you're actually opposing God. And what leader would want to step into the ring with God?

While there are times when, like one gunslinger confronting another, you may have to say, "There ain't room in town for both of us!" it's usually the last alternative. Instead, the better part of wisdom is to apply the next principle in helping others honestly assess their assumptions.

PRINCIPLE FOUR:

TO DISLODGE STRONGLY HELD POSITIONS, ASK PEOPLE TO DELAY JUDGMENT

Bringing about change is tough, because people tend to polarize around a position and hold to a perceived need to always be right. Rather than fighting it out at the "OK Corral," it's far better to delay making a judgment until additional questions have been addressed.

I find it fascinating that there were times when Jesus drew a line in the sand and told people that they were either with him or against him. On those occasions he left no middle ground. But there were also situations where he clearly took the time to interact with others and engage them in conversation.

The Man Who Met Jesus at Night

My favorite example is Nicodemus. The first and best-known meeting between Jesus and Nicodemus occurred one night when this religious leader told Jesus, "No one could perform the miraculous signs you are doing if God were not with him."[19] Instead of talking about his own identity as the Son of God, Jesus told this influential Pharisee how he could come to know God. Jesus explained that a person can only enter the kingdom of God by being born again.

Unlike the contentious encounters Jesus had with other Pharisees, the one with Nicodemus was tame. There's no indication that Jesus asked Nicodemus to make a decision to follow him at that time—but he did give the Pharisee plenty of food for thought.

Later, when some of the Pharisees were spewing venomous words about Jesus, Nicodemus asked, "Does our law condemn anyone without first hearing him to find out what he is doing?"[20] Nicodemus urged his colleagues to delay judgment, the very action he seems to have undertaken with respect to Jesus and his teachings.

After the crucifixion of Jesus it was Nicodemus who accompanied Joseph of Arimathea during the preparation of Jesus' body for burial.[21] Apparently Nicodemus had come at some point to the place where he could no longer delay a decision about Jesus; he accepted him as the Messiah, embracing the life-change that Jesus offered.

Forgo Judgment and Process Information

The delay in judgment was crucial because it allowed Nicodemus to further examine the words and works of Jesus. He was able to assess whether his previous assumptions about how a person could be made right with God were valid.

It's fascinating that in the face of intense social and religious pressure, Nicodemus was open to the possibility that he might be wrong. Instead of backing him into a corner Jesus gave him room to process and time to consider a viable alternative to his previously held assumptions.

Getting a hard-line opponent to be *open* to the possibility of another legitimate alternative is a major step in the direction of change. Instead of using the gunslinger approach, simply ask him or her to suspend their judgment. And indicate your own willingness to suspend judgment—after all, you may discover a new approach superior to the one you preferred.

> *The issue is not implementing a particular change, but creating an environment where people are comfortable with change. In that kind of environment change can be dynamic and life-giving.*

It's important to remember that the issue is not implementing a particular change, but creating an environment where people are comfortable with change—a setting where people see the benefit in challenging assumptions and the way things have always been done. In that kind of environment change can be dynamic and life-giving.

Miracles and Mystery

In the Grand Inquisitor section of Russian novelist Fyodor Dostoyevsky's extraordinary novel *The Brothers Karamazov*, the Grand Inquisitor was mad at Christ, insisting that he was only involved with miracles and mystery. Yet, quite frankly, I'm convinced the people you lead *want* to see more miracles and more mystery. Perhaps among the greatest miracles they'll behold will be the transformation in their own thinking as they learn to question long-held and deeply cherished assumptions and open their minds to the mystery of change.

THE WISDOM OF JESUS

- Jesus seized strategic opportunities to initiate change.

- Jesus described the future—in order to change the present.

- Jesus explained how a proposed change would support his vision.

- Jesus challenged assumptions—in order to reduce resistance to his ideas.

- Jesus continually asked questions.

- Jesus painted vivid word pictures aimed at undermining long-held assumptions.

- Jesus urged people to delay decisions.

13

PUT OTHERS FIRST

I have a confession to make: I did not pursue a leadership role because I believed it was the way I could best serve other people. It wasn't the thought of serving that captured my imagination, but a vision of the future and a desire to rally others around the vision so that together we could bring it into reality.

I hate to admit it, but the thought of serving others doesn't excite me. Consequently, if you're looking for a chapter on servant leadership written by someone who has arrived as a servant leader, well, you can move on now to the epilogue. By no means am I the expert on servant leadership. You see, part of me doesn't *want* to serve—in fact, I find the idea quite *unappealing*.

As I examine the life of Jesus I'm disturbed, no, not by him, but by the gap that separates me from him. You might think this isn't such an important issue—I know I've tried to convince myself it isn't. Yet, the greatest leader of all time—the possessor of unlimited power—used his extraordinary resources to *serve* others.

"How Can I Serve You?"

Jesus summed it up so simply yet so profoundly when he said, "The Son of Man did not come to be served, but to serve."[1] A short time after Jesus uttered those words he walked toward two blind men sitting by the side of a road.[2] When they heard it was Jesus passing by, they clamored for attention. The followers of Jesus acted like a maître d' in a five-star restaurant who had just heard a homeless person request a table with a view. They looked down their arrogant noses and told the blind men to be quiet.

The greatest leader of all time—the possessor of unlimited power—used his extraordinary resources to serve others.

Now Jesus could have passed by without a glance in their direction, and nobody would have given it a second thought. After all, why should a man with such unprecedented insight and such extraordinary power concern himself with a couple of "worthless" blind men?

Of course, Jesus didn't consider the men worthless at all, and he didn't quickly slip past them like we might do to a panhandler on a downtown street. Instead he stopped and asked, "What do you want me to do for you?"[3] In the final analysis, Jesus wanted to know how he could serve them. In essence, the leader of leaders asked two men who weren't even his regular followers, "How can I serve you?"

They in turn wanted the one thing that *only* Jesus could give them—their eyesight. In that moment a stirring of compassion happened inside Jesus that translated into a miracle of service and healing. The healing of these men wasn't simply an isolated incident in Jesus' life. *Every moment* of his life was spent serving others (bearing in mind, of course, that Jesus did on occasion break away from the crowds and spend time alone in order to restore his energy so he could serve more effectively later on).

176

Jesus' followers knew he was there to serve them. They understood that he always had their best interests at heart. Whether he was healing them, teaching them, feeding them, or rebuking them, they always knew he was seeking their highest good. Servant leadership wasn't just something Jesus did—it was the very essence of his being.

Wouldn't it be great if we could see this in Jesus and then immediately follow his lead! Unfortunately, Jesus' example doesn't have the same kind of instant effect on most of us that two extra-strength aspirin have on a headache. For a genuine change to occur in most of us, it will require more insight and a lot of practice. Like a pianist we'll need to gain understanding of the basic chords of servant leadership and then make ourselves practice them over and over. Over time it will become more natural for us—but I seriously doubt that we'll ever feel we've fully arrived. The greatest servant leaders I've known didn't see themselves as servants. I suspect they realized that even in their most humble moments there were traces of a self-serving motive still clinging to them like lint on a wool dinner jacket.

REACH FOR THE UNREACHABLE

When we speak of becoming servant leaders, we're striving for something we'll never quite grasp this side of heaven—like a kid on a merry-go-round reaching for a ring that's just beyond her grasp. But as we keep trying there will be moments when our fingertips will brush the surface of the ring—and we'll experience the miracle of Jesus working in us, empowering us to serve. If we become proud of ourselves, then the wonder will disappear, because our self-satisfaction will expose the sordid truth that we served only so we could see ourselves serving— like fans at a sporting event who realize they're on television and who wave vigorously so they can watch themselves on the big screen in the center of the arena.

Our aim is to put others first because we *genuinely* care for them—not because we want to be *seen* as caring for them.

Jesus can awaken such servant leadership in us as we strive to follow his example. While the principles in this chapter don't promise a quick fix, they will help us extend our reach, so that occasionally we will know that a miracle of service has happened in and through us.

Principle One:

Servant Leaders Are Motivated by Compassion

When the two blind men cried out to Jesus, the crowd saw them as intruders who needed to be silenced—irritants that needed to be brushed away like pesky flies. Jesus saw them in a radically different light. Matthew tells us that "Jesus had compassion on them."[4] Note that it was an internal response that preceded his actions. First Jesus felt compassion, and then he healed the men.

> *Our aim is to put others first because we genuinely care for them—not because we want to be seen as caring for them.*

On another occasion a man with leprosy approached Jesus, fell on his knees, and begged to be healed.[5] An awful disease, leprosy destroys the nervous system so that a man loses all sense of touch. If a diseased hand is cut, he won't feel pain. Unaware of the injury he won't protect the wound; infection may set in, resulting in the eventual loss of the hand. In its advanced stages the disease may have covered a man with pus-filled wounds and white shiny spots and could easily have caused the loss of a hand, arm, or leg.

Jesus Touched the Leper and Then Healed Him

A man with leprosy lived with the pain of constant rejection. Not only was he repulsive to look at, he was a social and religious outcast. Unlike contemporary AIDS patients, who can conceal their disease for many years, a man with leprosy had to make his illness known. According to ceremonial law he had to wear "torn clothes, let his hair be unkempt, cover the lower part of his face and cry out, 'Unclean! Unclean!'"[6] Anyone touched by a leper was immediately defiled by that momentary contact. As long as the man had leprosy, he had to live alone outside the city.

Instead of keeping his distance from Jesus, or warning him that he was unclean, the leprous man fell on his knees directly in front of him—in violation of all the cultural norms of that day. Mark tells us that in this situation Jesus was again "filled with compassion"[7] for the man. Again Jesus' internal response preceded the miracle of healing. Jesus identified with the man's heartache. He saw not someone who could defile him, someone he should keep at arm's length, but a lonely, suffering soul.

Motivated by compassion Jesus did the unthinkable. He touched the leper *and then* healed him. I would have performed the miracle first and then touched the man. But Jesus must have realized that the leper had not felt the warmth of a human touch in decades; he had not known the strength of an embrace in more years than he undoubtedly could remember. The man needed love more than he needed healing—he needed acceptance more than he needed cleansing.

The act of service flowed from a heart of compassion. Jesus calls us to follow his lead and to cultivate compassion for those under our charge. Frankly, my problem is I become so focused on bringing the dream into reality that I begin to view people impersonally. The destination becomes more important than the trip. When that happens, my ambition to succeed all too often squeezes compassion from my heart.

Listening Cultivates Compassion

Jesus did something I must force myself to do—he listened. I'm convinced that servant leaders are mastering the art of listening to what others say. They are embracing the prayer of Saint Francis of Assisi: "Lord, grant that I may not so much seek . . . to be understood as to understand."

Maybe you think you're too busy to slow down long enough to listen. But are you, really? Are your responsibilities more important than those of Jesus? Are the demands on your time greater?

I hope those questions trouble you, like they do me. You see, when we make excuses for our self-centered lifestyle, we're saying, "Because my arms are too short to reach the ring, I'll just get off the horse." You can do that—there's certainly nobody who is going to stop you. Indeed, many contemporary leaders have done just that—they've simply stopped trying to be servants.

You agree with me, don't you? Can't you think of numerous business, political, and religious leaders who have created an empire where others serve *them?* Haven't they built a kingdom where people are pawns in a chess game in which they make the rules—and rule number one is this: "Everyone is here for me."

Jesus stands in sharp contrast to such empire builders whose kingdoms will be forgotten before the headstone is placed over their grave. The greatest leader of all time didn't get so caught up in establishing God's kingdom that he neglected two blind men and a leper. It would be easy for us to view those encounters as a momentary, parenthetical lapse in leadership. It wasn't. Jesus didn't stop leading when he paused to listen to and to heal those men. Those passing encounters were leadership opportunities he could not let pass. By listening he was leading. By serving he was leading. Following his example begins with a heart of compassion, and compassion is cultivated through a listening ear.

Following Jesus' example begins with a heart of compassion, and compassion is cultivated through a listening ear.

PRINCIPLE TWO:

SERVANT LEADERS HONOR SECOND-STRING PLAYERS

I'm sure both the blind men and the leper were impressed not only that Jesus had healed their diseases, but also that he had healed *them*. They weren't like someone who wins the lottery because they're just plain lucky. Jesus had *chosen* to touch these men.

Jesus had an extraordinary aptitude for giving honor to second-string players. He consistently took time to honor "the little guy." On one occasion Jesus was mobbed by spectators and guarded by his disciples when several parents asked if he would touch their children. When Jesus' disciples rebuked the parents, he became indignant and said, "Let the little children come to me, and do not hinder them, for the kingdom of God belongs to such as these."[8] He then took the children in his arms, put his hands on them, and blessed them.

When Jesus blessed these children, he spoke well of them. In Old Testament times a blessing transferred a good thing from one person to another. When Isaac, under God's direction, blessed Jacob, he imparted the promise of bountiful crops, many servants, and a position of leadership in the family.[9] The words Jesus spoke imparted honor and dignity to the children he took in his arms.

The ABCs of Management

It's virtually impossible to measure the effect that words of praise from a leader have on a member of the team—especially on someone who never basks in the spotlight. In their book *Putting the One Minute Manager to Work*, Ken Blanchard and Robert Lorber reveal the ABCs of management:[10]

A = Activators	What a manager does *before* performance.
B = Behavior	Performance—what someone says or does.
C = Consequences ..	What a manager does *after* performance.

According to Blanchard and Lorber, most people think activators have a greater influence on future performance than do consequences. Yet, only fifteen to twenty-five percent of what influences performance comes from activators like goal-setting, while seventy-five to eighty-five percent of behavior comes from consequences like verbal affirmation.[11] A fundamental conclusion can be drawn from this research: If you want to maximize the effect of your words, catch people doing things right—and immediately praise them.

Because servant leaders realize that people have a deep need for affirmation, they go out of their way to praise *everyone* on the team—not just the impact players.

It's a Matter of Focus

I suppose you may be thinking, "Bill, that all sounds great, but you don't know the people on my team. There are a few I couldn't catch doing anything right if I watched them all day."

If you want to maximize the effect of your words, catch people doing things right—and immediately praise them.

I think the real issue here is one of focus, and not really one of reality. You will see what you look for, and you will get what you expect. Remember, the disciples saw the blind men, the leper, and the children as intruders; Jesus saw them as people he could serve. When we look for the good in others, we *will* see it, and in doing so we will find something to praise.

I'm reminded of the story about the man who volunteered to host the annual company party at his lakefront home. His wife loved to entertain, and so she quickly contacted the finest restaurant in town to cater the food and she located the best musicians to provide the music. On the day of the big event the weather was perfect, the food delicious, and the music upbeat.

As the crowd celebrated their good fortune to attend such a gala event at such a choice location, the hostess realized that she had forgotten to take care of a very important detail. Her daughter, Suzi, was a rambunctious seven-year-old who had a tendency to talk first and think later. The girl's mother hastily tracked her down and offered some specific instructions.

"Suzi, your dad's boss, Mr. Jones, will be here soon."

"I know," she said, looking around to see if he had arrived.

"And you know he has a veeeeeery large nose."

"I know. I've seen his picture, and his nose is bigger than Pinocchio's," she said, holding her hands several feet apart to indicate the length of Mr. Jones's nose.

"Dear, I don't want you to say anything to him about the size of his nose. Okay?"

"Of course not," Suzi said, insulted that her mother would suggest she might say such a thing. "That would hurt his feelings."

"Honey," her mother continued, "I don't want you to touch it or stare at it. When I introduce you, just say 'Hello' and then leave."

An hour or so later the hostess looked up and saw her daughter standing no more than five feet from Mr. Jones. She gasped, raced across the lawn, gently took Suzi by the hand, and said, "Mr. Jones, I'd like you to meet our daughter, Suzi.

"Suzi," she continued, "this is Mr. Jones, your father's boss."

The little girl shook the gentleman's hand and said, "It's good to meet you. I'm going inside to play with my computer. Good-bye."

As Suzi skipped off, the mother sighed in relief and said, "Mr. Jones, would you like me to fill your nose with coffee?"

This poor woman had been so focused on the size of Mr. Jones's nose it was all she could think about—and unfortunately, all she could talk about.

At one of the seminars I lead I sometimes place a single ink spot on a piece of white butcher paper and ask the audience what they see.

"A black spot," everyone says in unison.

It really happens that way—our eyes naturally focus on the black spots and ignore the white paper. Similarly, most of us tend to focus on what we perceive to be the negative characteristics in other people and ignore the positive; we see what people do wrong and miss what they do right. Servant leaders look for the good in others, and when they see it, they offer affirmation. The Bible does not tell us that Jesus commented on the runny noses, dirty hands, and ragged clothing of the children; it tells us that he took these precious children in his arms and spoke words of affirmation to them. He saw the good in each child and praised them for it.

PRINCIPLE THREE:

SERVANT LEADERS DO THE UNEXPECTED

My friend, author and educator Dr. Joe Aldrich, once noted that while every soul is equally precious to God, not every soul is equally strategic. There were many blind people and people with the disease of leprosy in ancient Israel whom Jesus didn't heal. There were thousands of children he didn't bless. Most of the people Jesus healed had only a fleeting encounter with him—like a baseball fan who gets a star player's autograph after a game. While many of those who were healed may have followed Jesus, they remained only in the outer circle of influence.

The successful outcome of Jesus' mission would not rest on these men and women, but on the dozen he had chosen from the masses—twelve men he had selected to be strategic leaders (another seventy-two made up the second circle of influence—see Luke 10:1, but less is known about them).

As leaders we must constantly serve members of the team whose influence is limited—men and women who make up the rank and file. But we must also serve strategic leaders in the same way—as we cultivate compassion by listening and offer encouragement by speaking timely words of affirmation. At the same time, we do well to serve strategic leaders in ways they don't expect.

Surprise Them by Serving

What does it mean to serve leaders in *unexpected* ways? I believe such service is unexpected because leaders are typically seen as masters, not as servants. The man who supervises the company parking facility doesn't expect the chief executive officer to show personal interest in him by asking about his family. And a junior executive doesn't expect the CEO to visit his wife in the hospital after the birth of their first child. The woman who delivers mail to the executive offices every day doesn't expect the president of the company to remember her birthday. Nor does a new regional manager expect the company's president to unexpectedly show up at an athletic event her son or daughter is playing in. The larger the organization the more insulated people expect the leader to be. Jesus repeatedly proved he was the consummate servant leader by his willingness to do the unexpected.

The most memorable example occurred on the night before his crucifixion. The disciples hadn't been in the upper room long before an argument broke out as to which of them was the greatest.[12] While the men compared credentials and résumés, they were waiting for a servant to wash their feet. The job wasn't a desirable one, and it was customarily carried out by a low-ranking slave.

None of the disciples expected Jesus to take off his robe, wrap a towel around his waist, fill the basin with water, and begin to gently clean their feet.[13] That was a job no leader ever did—at least it was a job no *master* leader ever did. But Jesus was a servant leader, and that's exactly what he did.

It's not hard to imagine the embarrassment that must have painted every man's face red. While Jesus didn't initially utter a single word, his actions spoke volumes. The towel, the water, the hands cradling twenty-four dirty feet (including Judas's feet) all shouted out, "You want to see greatness? Here it is—the leader of leaders washing the dirty feet of his team. Now *that's* greatness!"

Peter was so offended that he initially refused to let Jesus wash his feet. Yet maybe "offended" is the wrong word. Peter might not have been offended at all. It's possible, I suppose, that he tried to take advantage of the situation by *appearing* to be offended so Jesus would view him as the one disciple who truly understood servanthood. Perhaps he hoped that his refusal would assure him of the top spot in the kingdom—the one they had been so vehemently arguing about before Jesus began to wash their feet.

While we'll never know Peter's motives, we do know that Jesus made it clear that Peter *would* allow him to wash his feet—or Peter would have to find the nearest exit. Given that choice, Peter watched in silent awe as the One he knew had created the world washed his dirty feet.

Surprise Them with a Towel, Not Fireworks

It fascinates me that on the last evening of his life here on earth, at a time when Jesus needed to impress his followers with the most important aspects of his work, he didn't remind them of all the flashy things he had done. He didn't review how many people had been healed, fed, taught, forgiven, or raised from the dead. He didn't talk about walking on the water or driving out demons. Jesus didn't perform a few private miracles to serve as final reminders of his supernatural power. There was no transfiguration where he allowed his shining glory to peek through his robe. He didn't give them a sort of grand finale—like the conclusion of the Fourth of July fireworks display—to wow them.

On the last evening of his life here on earth, Jesus didn't remind his disciples of all the flashy things he had done. Instead, he quietly, humbly washed their feet.

Instead, Jesus quietly, humbly washed their feet. And then he said, "I have set you an example that you should do as I have done for you."[14] Jesus didn't tell his disciples to "do *what* I have done," but to "do *as* I have done." He's not necessarily calling his followers to literally wash each other's feet—but he *is* calling them to be servant leaders. And the example he used to deliver that call was as unexpected as a snowflake on a summer day in Texas.

Surprise Them by Yielding

I think the problem many of us have with servant leadership is that we see it as a sign of weakness when it is in actuality a sign of strength. We fail to recognize that it requires more internal strength, more strength of character, to serve than to be served. The Chinese philosopher Laotzu wrote in 600 B.C.:

> Water is fluid, soft, and yielding. But water will wear away rock, which is rigid and cannot yield. As a rule, whatever is fluid, soft, and yielding will overcome whatever is rigid and hard. This is another paradox: what is soft is strong.[15]

Jesus demonstrated extraordinary strength and self-control when he accepted the role of a servant. It requires significantly more self-control to use our power for others than for ourselves. Before Jesus washed the disciples' feet, John noted something that gives us insight into the source of Jesus' strength. This is what John wrote: "Jesus knew that the Father had put all things under his power, and that he had come from God and was returning to God."[16]

Jesus knew who he was, where he had come from, and where he was going. That kind of self-awareness meant that Jesus had nothing to prove. He could use his incomparable power to *serve* because, unlike the disciples, he wasn't vying for influence and recognition.

Surprise Them with Grace

Not too long ago I had lunch with a friend who had just resigned as the president of an influential West Coast bank. Over the period of eight years Vic had led the bank through a cycle of explosive growth—when he left, the bank was ten times its original size.

Vic had been a leader in a church I had served as pastor almost a decade ago. Toward the end of my ministry there I lost a power struggle that ended in my resignation. I vividly remember Vic and several other influential people pleading with me to let them initiate a battle they believed would ultimately result in gaining the support of the congregation. Vic and I had had a phone conversation that went something like this:

"So you want to fight it out?" I asked.

"Yes," he said.

"In the past we always managed to win the important debates [some of them were more like barroom brawls than debates], didn't we?"

"Yes," he said.

"And when those who had lost stirred up dissension, what did we know about them?"

"We knew they weren't following the lead of Jesus," he said.

"If they had followed his lead, they would have supported the decision, even though they disagreed with it, right?"

"Right."

"Have the rules changed now that we're on the losing end?" I asked.

"This is hard," he said softly.

"I know. But, Vic, if my life has had any influence on you over the last nine years, then leave it alone. We show greater strength by submitting than by fighting, because by walking away we show that Jesus rules our lives."

That conversation took place almost ten years ago, and I hadn't thought about it again until the day Vic and I met over lunch. It was then that he told me that this exchange had profoundly influenced his leadership style. "In the course of managing the bank there have been many battles," he said. "I never forgot your willingness to step aside rather than use your influence destructively. You could have brought those who sought your ruin to their knees. You could have fought for the reins of power. Instead, you served your opponents by graciously walking away."

I have to admit I look back on that decision with mixed feelings. Walking away from a compelling vision that was supported by millions of dollars in resources and many friends wasn't easy (moreover, as a former street-fighter I cringe at the thought of walking away from a fight). But to this day I know it was the right thing to do, because I know it's what Jesus would have done.

When a leader's identity is wrapped up in God—not in their own achievement, power, fame, or wealth—they're liberated from the baneful striving after these things. Once this liberation occurs, the strength of Jesus will flow through them, because, like him, they are serving those under their charge.

While there are still battles that must be fought, servant leaders fight not to exalt *themselves*, but to advance a just and good cause. Such men and women know how to win with humility and lose with grace. In the process they impart to those they lead something infinitely more important than victory—they impart the life of Jesus, which, like a baton in a relay race, can be passed on in turn to the next runner and on to the next and the next ...

> *When a leader's identity is wrapped up in God—not in their own achievement, power, fame, or wealth—they're liberated from the baneful striving after these things.*

∞

The Wisdom of Jesus

- Jesus asked, "How can I serve you?"

- Jesus didn't just carry out servant leadership—it was the essence of his being.

- Jesus felt compassion for those he served.

- Jesus did the unthinkable.

- Jesus listened.

- Jesus honored second-string players.

- Jesus saw the good in others and praised them for it.

- Jesus did the unexpected.

- Jesus surprised his team by serving them.

- Jesus served with grace.

EPILOGUE

*W*ay back, at the very beginning of this book, I noted that each of us is like a plane leaving an airport—a two-percent change in trajectory at takeoff in Los Angeles will take us to a radically different place two thousand miles away. What is true of planes is true of you. A small change in the way you think and act will enable you to take those you lead to a better place over the course of a year.

In the process of reading this book there must have been some thoughts that resonated with you. You may have read an insight or two and said to yourself, "Oh yeah! If I did that I'd be a better leader!"

The secret to implementing successful change in your life is to focus on less, not more. Don't try to do too much. Focus on those specific insights that resonated with you—and diligently apply them. Read and reread those chapters, or portions of chapters, that hit home with you. Mark up those pages and read from them so frequently that they become tattered. Share the insights with your spouse, children, coworkers, and friends. Every time you tell someone what you've learned you'll not only be helping them, you'll be helping yourself by reviewing and owning what you've learned.

Oh, and yes, there is yet one other thing you'll want to remember. There's a miraculous and supernatural element involved in following Jesus' example. You see, Jesus does more than point the way for you to follow. Unlike other great leaders, he seeks a relationship with you. He wants to empower you to be a better leader. Imagine ... the greatest leader of all time offers you more than his wisdom; he offers you himself! As you apply his wisdom and tap into his power, you'll discover others doing what you want them to do, not because you told them to, but because they want to.

AWAKEN THE LEADER WITHIN
DISCUSSION GUIDE

This discussion guide is provided as a way for you to dig deeper into the issues raised and the insights shared in *Awaken the Leader Within*. You will benefit from using these questions and prompts for individual study and, perhaps even more so, from using them for study within a team or a small group. Becoming a leader who learns daily from the wisdom of Jesus will take more than a desire; a team or a small group can provide you with not only additional insights but with the elements of accountability, discipline, and authenticity that will help awaken the leader within you.

Chapter 1: Turn Your Potential Loose

1. If leadership is getting others to do what you want them to do because they want to do it, who are the people you lead?

2. Why is it important to view leadership as an art rather than as an inherited ability?

3. How did Jesus view the relationship between character and competence in a leader? How does this affect the development of the leader within you?

Chapter 2: Wear No Masks

1. In what areas of your life do you possess sterling integrity? Why is it possible for you to demonstrate integrity in these areas and not in other areas?

2. Identify an area where you differ on the inside from the way you appear on the outside. If this is difficult for you, listen carefully over the next couple of days to promises you make and explanations you give. See how closely they line up with reality. Look for occasions where you exaggerate.

Note how willing you are to assume responsibility for mistakes you've made.

3. Once you've identified an area where you need to bring your ethic and your behavior into alignment, make this discrepancy a matter of daily prayer.

Chapter 3: Look Ahead

1. Do you know your core values? When you reflect on them, does something inside you say, "Yeah, that's what's important to me"? If you're not sure what your core values are, take some time and write out the values you deeply believe to be true. Encourage those on your team to do the same thing. Share the results of your reflections, and try to merge them into a handful of core values. To give you an idea of what a core value looks like when it's written out, here are some from our church:

    -   Authenticity—cultivating an honest relationship with God and others, and dealing candidly with ourselves individually about who we are and what we're going through.

    -   Creativity—using the arts with excellence to communicate truth, build bridges, and facilitate worship.

    -   Safety—accepting one another as God accepts us and entering into relationships that reflect his unconditional love.

2. Have you answered the question, "Why am I here?" I mean this not in some theological sense, but in the sense of, "Have you discovered your destiny? Can you articulate why God placed you on the earth so that when your life is over, you'll know if you finished the job he gave you to do?"

Ask God to give you the wisdom needed to find out. After you've pondered these questions for a time, write out a brief purpose statement for yourself and the group you lead. Then read the purpose statement and ask why. Now, rewrite it and ask why again. Before long you will have narrowed down your purpose statement.

3. Take a time-out and go alone to a place of solitude. Urge the leaders on your team to do the same thing. Answer the question, "If time and resources were of no consequence, what would my future look like?" Describe a *Blow Your Socks Off Vision* that excites you about the future. Next, have the key members of your team share their *Blow Your Socks Off Vision* with the rest of the team. Once you've done that, you'll be encouraged by the energy it generates and the positive results that are produced.

4. Buy a copy of *Built to Last* by James Collins and Jerry Porras. I tip my hat to them for the numerous insights I have gleaned from their book and have gratefully put to use in this chapter. It's the best book I've read on the subject of visionary leadership. Get yourself a copy, and read it through slowly.

Chapter 4: Lead the Charge

1. In what ways have you exercised courage as a leader?

2. If you asked those you lead to answer the above question, what do you think they would say?

3. What lessons have you learned from past failures? In what ways can you see that the law of success has proven true for you? How can you apply this law to a current challenge so that it gives you courage?

4. Identify an upcoming decision where you can ask the question, "How does my saying yes in this situation support my core values and driving purpose?" How does it bolster your courage to ask that question?

5. What are you currently doing to better prepare yourself to be an effective leader? What can you do in the future?

CHAPTER 5: DEPEND ON GOD

1. How reliable have you been when it comes to your daily meeting with God? What could you do to improve your track record in this area? Can you list a few reasons why committing to a daily meeting with God would be a good idea? How might even a five-minute meeting strengthen your faith? (I encourage leaders to start with a time slot they can keep and then build on it.)

2. What are your greatest fears? What does the wisdom of Jesus tell you about how to face them?

3. Is there something you're holding on to that is hindering your relationship with God? What steps can you take to release it?

4. If you were to follow the example of Jesus in your relationship with God, what would change?

CHAPTER 6: FINISH WHAT YOU START

1. Did you count the cost before entering into your current leadership role? If you were to do so now, how would you change your evaluation of the cost?

2. Can you point to a situation in the past where you wish you hadn't given up? What lessons have you learned from that experience that will give you courage in your present leadership role?

3. What situations cause you to sometimes want to leave your current post? As you make your approach to the four "traffic lights" mentioned in this chapter, what color are they?

4. What single attitudinal change can you make that will enable you to show diligence and follow-through as a leader? How will that change affect those you lead?

CHAPTER 7: BRIDLE YOUR APPETITES

1. Why is it so dangerous to nurture a pet sin?

2. What can you do to protect yourself from your area of weakness?

3. Once you've answered question two, share your answer with a friend.

4. What are the three elements that will help you bridle your appetites? How can each one aid *you*?

CHAPTER 8: KEEP THE VISION ALIVE

1. Think of three different settings where you can help those you lead focus on the vision of the organization. Identify two situations where Jesus adapted his vision to the people he was talking with.

2. Do others view you as an optimist or a pessimist? What can you do to become more optimistic? In what ways can you turn mistakes or failures into opportunities for growth?

3. What role does preparation have in inspiring others to a shared vision? What can you do to be more prepared while raising your team's own level of preparation?

CHAPTER 9: FLESH OUT YOUR VALUES

1. If you haven't done so yet, write out your personal and organizational core values. Use them to help you make decisions by asking, "Does this decision express my core values?" Specify how it fleshes out your core values.

2. If you haven't done so yet, write out your personal and organizational driving purpose. Use this statement to help you make decisions by asking, "Does this decision advance my driving purpose?" Articulate how it does or doesn't.

3. Make a commitment to incorporate two kinds of prayer into your decision-making process. Before important decisions devote a significant chunk of time to pray for wisdom. Ask God to provide you with the information and counsel you need to help you make the wisest decision. At regular intervals throughout the day briefly connect with God regarding all the issues that arise and require a decision of one kind or another.

198

CHAPTER 10: DEVELOP *WE-ISM*

1. In what ways do you practice *me-ism*? How can you cultivate a spirit of *we-ism* within yourself and those on your

team? Brainstorm with your team about how each member can put the team first.

2. Have each member of your team describe how his or her particular role helps fulfill the vision of the team.

3. Make it your goal to cast the vision with someone on your team every day this week.

4. Talk with your team about the ways they sacrifice in order to see the vision become a reality. Give them affirmation for their willingness to do so.

5. Develop a strategy to help your team achieve higher levels of excellence. Brainstorm about how you can achieve a balance between accountability and a freedom to fail.

CHAPTER 11: KEEP THE TEAM UNITED

1. Do others view you as approachable? Why or why not?

2. What ineffective methods of conflict management did you learn while growing up?

3. What can you do to obey the command of Jesus and treat your enemies with generosity and love?

4. What steps can you take to help your team learn the importance of dealing with conflict personally?

5. Is there anyone to whom you need to apologize and ask for forgiveness? Is there someone *you* need to forgive?

6. How can you help your team apply the principles of conflict resolution taught and modeled by Jesus?

Chapter 12: Be a Change Master

1. On a scale of 1–10 how would you rate yourself as a vision caster? What could you do to raise your score?

2. How do the changes you want to implement support the core values of the organization you lead? How will they help bring the vision into reality?

3. Today begin creating an environment where everybody vigorously challenges all assumptions. Make *why* one of the most frequently heard words at your leadership meetings.

4. Identify the assumptions behind the resistance you're encountering as you try to implement change. How can you help those who hold the assumptions assess their validity?

5. The next time you challenge someone's assumption, use a vivid word picture to open others up to the value of a reassessment.

6. Instead of fighting it out with those who most vigorously resist your proposed changes, ask them to reserve judgment. Provide them with the information they need to intelligently evaluate their assumptions. At the same time they assess their assumptions, be sure to do the same with yours.

7. I'm indebted to Edward de Bono for his insights concerning creative thinking. I'd strongly urge you and your team members to read his book, *Lateral Thinking: Creativity Step by Step*, published by HarperCollins in a reissue edition (1990).

CHAPTER 13: PUT OTHERS FIRST

1. When you see someone under your charge struggling with a problem, do you respond with impatience, or with compassion? How can you cultivate compassion? How does listening cultivate compassion?

2. Identify some specific ways you can honor some of the second-string players on your team.

3. How can you unexpectedly serve your team?

4. What is the value of servant leadership?

5. How did Jesus serve his disciples? What attitude enabled him to serve them even as they were arguing about who was the greatest?

NOTES

CHAPTER 2: WEAR NO MASKS

1. James M. Kouzes and Barry Z. Posner, *Credibility: How Leaders Gain and Lose It, Why People Demand It* (San Francisco: Jossey-Bass, 1993), 14.
2. Hebrews 13:8
3. *Webster's College Dictionary*, 2^d ed. (New York: Random House, 1997), 679.
4. Matthew 4:19–20
5. Philip Van Doren Stern, ed., *The Life and Writings of Abraham Lincoln* (New York: Random House, 1999), 226.
6. Matthew 5:17
7. John 8:46
8. The story is told in an article by Carolyn White titled, "Real Nick Eddy Forgives Fake One," *USA Today* (October 8, 1999), C7.
9. John 14:9
10. Matthew 16:16
11. Matthew 26:35
12. Luke 22:32
13. John 21:3
14. John 21:15–19
15. See Galatians 2:11–16, where Paul takes Peter to task for his hypocrisy.
16. Matthew 23:27–28

CHAPTER 3: LOOK AHEAD

1. Proverbs 15:1
2. James C. Collins and Jerry I. Porras, *Built to Last* (New York: HarperCollins, 1997), 222.
3. Matthew 22:36
4. Matthew 22:37–39
5. Mark 11:15–18
6. John 11:35
7. Matthew 27:45–50

8. Collins and Porras, *Built to Last*, 225.

9. John 17:1, 4

10. Luke 19:10

11. Matthew 4:1–11

12. James M. Strock, *Reagan on Leadership* (Rocklin, Calif.: Prima Publishing, 1998), 29.

13. Genesis 1:26–27

14. Sheila Murray Bethel, *Making a Difference* (New York: Berkley Publishing, 1990), 44.

15. John 14:1–3

16. Matthew 19:28

17. Matthew 19:30

18. Luke 1:52

19. Luke 1:53

CHAPTER 4: LEAD THE CHARGE

1. Matthew 6:33

2. John 12:24

3. M. Scott Peck, *The Road Less Traveled* (New York: Simon & Schuster, 1978), 15.

4. Pat Riley, *The Winner Within* (New York: Berkley Publishing, 1993), 106.

5. Luke 9:1–6

6. Luke 9:13–14

7. Don Shula and Ken Blanchard, *Everyone's a Coach* (New York: Harper Business/Grand Rapids: Zondervan, 1995), 82.

8. Adapted from Bill Perkins, *When Good Men Are Tempted* (Grand Rapids: Zondervan, 1997), 116.

9. John 14:18

10. Exodus 3:12

11. Joshua 1:1–9

12. Quoted in Clifton Fadiman, gen. ed., *The Little Brown Book of Anecdotes* (Boston: Little, Brown and Company, 1985), 302.

CHAPTER 5: DEPEND ON GOD

1. Mark 1:35

2. Mark 6:46

3. Luke 6:12
4. Mark 14:34
5. Mark 14:35
6. Matthew 26:36–46
7. Hebrews 5:7–10
8. Hebrews 5:7
9. Luke 22:44
10. Quoted in Alan Loy McGinnis, *The Friendship Factor* (Minneapolis: Augsburg, 1979), 28.
11. Matthew 26:39, 42, 44
12. Matthew 26:39–44

CHAPTER 6: FINISH WHAT YOU START

1. Luke 14:33
2. Luke 8:26–39
3. Luke 8:39
4. John 14:1–2
5. John 14:3
6. Luke 22:31–32
7. James 1:2–4
8. Luke 22:32
9. James 1:2

CHAPTER 7: BRIDLE YOUR APPETITES

1. Matthew 6:13
2. Matthew 6:24
3. Romans 6:16
4. Luke 22:31, 54–62
5. Matthew 4:1–11
6. 1 Corinthians 10:18–20
7. Matthew 8:8
8. Matthew 12:35
9. James 1:14–15; see discussion in Perkins, *When Good Men Are Tempted*, 123-33
10. Matthew 6:24
11. John 17:20–21
12. John 14:18
13. Matthew 28:20
14. John 15:5

CHAPTER 8: KEEP THE VISION ALIVE

1. James Kouzes and Barry Posner, *The Leadership Challenge* (San Francisco: Jossey-Bass, 1988), 109.
2. The story is told in an article by Susan Vaughn, *Investor's Business Daily* (June 4, 1999), A5.
3. Matthew 4:19
4. Luke 5:32
5. John 4:35
6. Luke 19:10
7. Luke 8:1–12
8. Matthew 5:14–16
9. Quoted in the article "UPS Founder Jim Casey," *Investor's Business Daily* (October 20, 1999), A4.
10. John 8:1–11
11. John 8:10–11
12. Luke 10:17
13. Luke 10:23–24
14. The story is told in Jack Cranfield and Mark Victor Hansen, *Chicken Soup for the Soul* (Deerfield Beach, Fla.: Health Communications, 1993), 214–17.
15. Matthew 4:1–11

CHAPTER 9: FLESH OUT YOUR VALUES

1. Quoted in Bethel, *Making a Difference*, 148–49.
2. Matthew 6:24
3. Matthew 8:22
4. Luke 8:20
5. Luke 8:21
6. Matthew 12:22–24
7. Quoted in Bethel, *Making a Difference*, 67.
8. Luke 6:12–16
9. Matthew 14:29

CHAPTER 10: DEVELOP *WE-ISM*

1. Matthew 20:20–28
2. John 17:20–21
3. John 17:22–23
4. Matthew 16:28

5. Matthew 17:2
6. Matthew 24–25
7. Matthew 24:36–25:46
8. Matthew 25:24–30
9. Matthew 14:28–30
10. Matthew 14:13–21
11. Matthew 17:14–21
12. Matthew 26:69–75
13. Matthew 26:47–56

CHAPTER 11: KEEP THE TEAM UNITED

1. Quoted in Charles R. Swindoll, *The Quest for Character* (Grand Rapids: Zondervan, 1993), 35–36.
2. Exodus 21:24; see also Leviticus 24:20; Deuteronomy 19:21; Matthew 5:38
3. Matthew 5:39
4. Matthew 5:44
5. Matthew 5:45
6. Matthew 5:45
7. Matthew 5:44
8. John 15:1–8
9. Lee Iacocca with William Novak, *Iacocca: An Autobiography* (New York: Bantam, 1984), 111.
10. Matthew 5:23–24
11. Matthew 18:15
12. Matthew 4:1–11
13. See Matthew 15:16, for example
14. Matthew 16:23
15. Matthew 18:1–9; 20:20–28; Luke 22:24–30
16. Matthew 23:1–39
17. Quoted in McGinnis, *The Friendship Factor*, 148–49.
18. Luke 17:5
19. Luke 17:6

CHAPTER 12: BE A CHANGE MASTER

1. This quote and the others in this paragraph are taken from Tom Peters, *The Tom Peters Seminar* (New York: Vintage Books, 1994), 9–10.

2. Jeanenne LaMarsh, *Changing the Way We Change* (Reading, Mass.: Addison-Wesley, 1995), 1.

3. From "Julius Caesar," act 4, scene 3, quoted in David McNally, *Even Eagles Need a Push* (New York: Dell, 1990), 223.

4. Matthew 5–7

5. Matthew 5:3–12

6. Matthew 5:13–7:27

7. Matthew 17:1–8

8. Quoted in Warren Bennis, *Herding Cats* (Provo, Utah: Executive Excellence, 1999), 154–55.

9. Matthew 16:22

10. Mark 6:5

11. Luke 15

12. Matthew 15:2

13. Matthew 15:3–9

14. Edward de Bono, *Lateral Thinking* (New York: Harper & Row, 1973), 91.

15. De Bono, *Lateral Thinking*, 93.

16. Luke 5:33

17. Luke 5:34–35

18. Luke 5:37–38

19. John 3:2

20. John 7:51

21. John 19:38–42

CHAPTER 13: PUT OTHERS FIRST

1. Matthew 20:28

2. Matthew 20:29–34

3. Matthew 20:32

4. Matthew 20:34

5. Mark 1:40–45

6. Leviticus 13:45

7. Mark 1:41

8. Mark 10:14

9. Genesis 27:27–29

10. Robert Lorber and Kenneth Blanchard, *Putting the One Minute Manager to Work* (New York: Simon & Schuster, 1995).

11. Quoted in Zig Ziglar, *Top Performance* (New York: Berkley Publishing, 1986), 47–48.

12. Luke 22:24–30

13. John 13:3–5

14. John 13:15

15. Quoted in Bethel, *Making a Difference,* 168.

16. John 13:3

We want to hear from you. Please send your comments about this book to us in care of the address below. Thank you.

ZondervanPublishingHouse

Grand Rapids, Michigan 49530

http://www.zondervan.com